Rejection Free for Authors.

More Bestselling Titles From
Scott Allan

Empower Your Thoughts

Empower Your Deep Focus

Rejection Reset

Rejection Free

Relaunch Your Life

Drive Your Destiny

The Discipline of Masters

Do the Hard Things First

Undefeated

No Punches Pulled

Fail Big

Bite the Bullet

Supercharge Your Best Life

Built for Stealth

Visit author.to/ScottAllanBooks to follow Scott Allan and stay up to date on future book releases

JOIN THE COMMUNITY OF 30,000 LIFETIME LEARNERS!

Sign up today for my **free weekly newsletter** and receive instant access to **the <u>onboarding subscriber pack</u>** that includes:

The Fearless Confidence Action Guide: _9 Action Plans for Building Limitless Confidence and Achieving Sustainable Results!_

The bestseller poster pack: _A poster set of Scott Allan's bestselling books_

The Zero Procrastination Blueprint: _A Step-by-Step Blueprint to Turn Procrastination into Rapid Action Implementation!_

**Begin Your Journey and Make This Life Your Own.
Click Here to <u>Subscribe Today</u>, or scan the <u>QR code</u> below.**

Rejection
FREE

For Authors

How to Conquer Writer's Rejection, Crush Your Inner Critic,
and Fearlessly Publish Your Book

By Scott Allan

ISBN (Paperback): 978-1-990484-52-0

ISBN (eBook): 978-1-990484-51-3

ISBN (Hardcover): 978-1-989599-38-9

CONTENTS

"It took me fifteen years to discover I had no talent for writing, but I couldn't give it up because by that time I was too famous."

— Robert Benchley

Dedication

For those struggling authors who still fight to believe in their craft, the **struggle within** is the only one you have to pay attention to.

This book is for *you*.

Foreword: By Derek Doepker

There's a word for people who hate rejection—**human**.

As human beings, we're psychologically hardwired to want to fit in with the tribe. You can tell yourself all day long not to care what other people think and that rejection doesn't matter. It won't change the underlying emotional resistance that's there whenever you endeavor to do anything that puts you out there for potential rejection.

This means you won't need to eliminate the fear of rejection. It's not a moral failing if you've found yourself concerned with the opinions of others. The key to overcoming resistance to rejection isn't "not caring" about what others think.

Rather, the solution is to develop such a commitment to your craft and to those you serve that the sting of rejection won't derail you. In the same way one might run into a burning building to save a child, you'll take the heat of the haters out of love for your true fans.

If you're not getting rejected a lot, you're not reaching a lot of people. Which means fear of rejection will forever hold you back from your potential until you break through it. I've worked with thousands of authors. Many were given the best strategies in the world, but they wouldn't apply them fully because something deep inside held them back.

Often, it's a deeper fear of rejection. No marketing book or tactics will help them until they do the deeper work that this book discusses.

The funny thing about rejection is that it can be seen as an illusion, or it can be seen as inevitable.

It's inevitable when you realize that no matter what you put out there, someone isn't going to like it. And if someone decides not to publish their book, then they're rejecting themselves before anyone else has a chance to.

No matter what, rejection happens.

On the other hand, you may discover rejection is just an illusion. Imagine being a server at a cocktail party. Some may greatly appreciate what you're offering. Others may not care for what's on your plate. Do you feel rejected when they decline what you're offering, or do you simply move along until you find someone who appreciates it? It may not seem like rejection at all.

I find this to be a good analogy. As an author, you are in the service industry. You are in service to others by providing entertainment or education. If you hold back your service because some might reject it, how many people would be robbed of your gifts?

You must break through any concerns of rejection not only for your own fulfillment, but also for the fulfillment of those who are starving for your work.

There is another way of seeing rejection as well. You can see it as a gift. The more you endure rejection and come through it, the more emotionally resilient you'll be. The saying "building thick skin" applies well. If you want thicker skin, you must stress the skin to build callouses. It takes real-world effort and discomfort to toughen your emotional skin.

It's one thing to know that you will go through rejection and need to develop a thick skin as an author. What you've probably found, though, is that intellectually knowing isn't enough. You need to feel an even stronger inner conviction and courage. You need a visceral experience of breaking through those old doubts and fears to experience yourself now as a bold and daring creative.

That's what this book is for. Scott's insights will help you develop the emotional strength and resilience you need to boldly face rejection, move through it, and emerge stronger for having endured it.

This means you must implement what's in this book because it's through implementation that you gain the emotional charge you need to go from thinking to embodying.

Read this book, apply what you learn, transform yourself, and then go transform the world with your writing.

— *Derek Doepker*

Derek Doepker is the #1 Bestselling Author of Why Authors Fail, Break Through Your BS, and The Healthy Habit Revolution. He is committed to empowering people to reach their fullest potential and escape the dangerous trap of mediocrity.

Introduction: Rejection Free for **Authors**

"Writing a book is a horrible, exhausting struggle, like a long bout of some painful illness. One would never undertake such a thing if one were not driven on by some demon whom one can neither resist nor understand."

—George Orwell

Do you dream of becoming a writer but you can't get past that fear of being rejected by critics? Are you afraid of hitting the publish button because of what others might think? Do you struggle to explain why you write?

Whether you are an aspiring author or a seasoned veteran in publishing, confronting criticism and rejection is the most fearful aspect for many writers. The experience of sitting down to create a story, novel, or nonfiction piece is both exhilarating and frightening.

As storytellers, teachers, and leaders we take a lot of pride in the work we produce. When it gets a bad review or readers publicly criticize it, we may feel discouraged enough to give up.

If you want to become a successful author, dealing with the pressure of rejection and criticism is a real fear. Those who persevere with extreme resilience are the successful writers who make a real business out of their art.

If you have the desire to write, but you're held back by the blank page syndrome, or you can't get past the fear of being rejected or criticized, this book is for you.

I wrote this book for aspiring authors—both young and old—so we can join forces to battle the killer of dreams. This enemy is self-doubt and fear, and it's alive in our work as writers.

Whether you are new to writing and publishing, or have already published multiple books, you could be struggling with fears that hold you back from attaining total satisfaction in your work. I could offer age-old advice, such as, "Don't worry about what others think. Just do it!"

However, we tend to get stuck and we *do* care what others think. If you are thinking about writing or have been writing for years, you will benefit from the guidance *Rejection Free for Writers* can offer you.

This book isn't about pleasing others. It is about dealing with your inner struggle: combating the rejection and self-doubt that plagues your mind when you sit in front of the blank page.

When it comes to rejection, we have all been there before. We've been rejected in love, rejected by kids at school, or rejected by employers. We know how it feels. It hurts and we want to avoid that pain. But avoiding it is not the solution. Confronting your fears, crushing self-doubt, and taking massive action toward your craft is the formula for winning.

If you want to destroy that fear and write the book you have been dreaming about for years, you are in the right place.

To succeed, we must toughen up so that nothing gets in the way of what we're setting out to accomplish. You want to write a book, but you can't find a way to start? You wrote your first draft and now you don't know what to do? You need to market your book, but you're afraid of reaching out to influencers? I can relate to all of that.

In the years I have been writing, it has been difficult to overcome the many challenges in the publishing field: Writing good material, marketing it to an audience, and trying to stay on top of all the tasks that come with building a book business. As tough as this has been, the most challenging has been facing my own fears and limitations. The doubts I had about my writing skills. Not knowing if my efforts would pay off. Afraid to ask for help because I felt like a nobody.

In *Rejection Free For Writers,* I can give you the strategies and confidence to do what you need to do to get to the final stage and publish your book.

In this book, you will learn how to:

- Get over the fear of writing that first page.

- Understand the psychology of rejection and how it impacts you as an author.

- Stop the comparison game and be the creative author you've always wanted to be.

- Develop strategies for managing your time.

- Become more transparent and reach your audience.

- Write what you love.

- Build an author identity.

- Overcome the self-doubt keeping you stuck.

- Control your perfectionistic ways.

- Punch out your inner critic when it gets too loud.

- Live up to and exceed your own expectations as an author.

- Gain confidence to present yourself as a professional writer.

- Create your writing routine for greater productivity.

- Learn to deal with critics and reviews.

- Fearlessly market yourself to sell more books.

- Make writing a daily habit so you can build up your confidence and create a powerful passive income funnel.

The purpose of this book is to teach you how to handle rejection as a writer. I will also cover the strategies for dealing with critics and, how to build your craft into a passion you can share with your readers and the world.

A Vision for Your Writing

By the time you are finished *Rejection Free for Writers*, you'll be writing like mad without worrying whether your material is any good or not. Of course it's good, and you deserve to share it.

But first I want you to sit back and close your eyes for five minutes. Find a nice quiet place where you can be alone with your thoughts. You're going to do a visualization exercise. It's lots of fun—trust me.

For five minutes, imagine that you're a successful writer. You have a published book, or a series of books. Your fans are eagerly waiting for the next release. How would you spend your time every day? What would you create? What are people saying about your latest book? Go deeply into this vision of the life you could be leading if you were doing what you love as a part-time/full-time author.

Maybe you don't want to be a full-time writer, but you want to market yourself better, connect with people more fluently, and be in a position in which obstacles such as fear or doubt no longer hold you back. Anything is possible when you believe in yourself and your passion for the written word.

Imagine where would you be if you could navigate through the self-rejection, fear, and doubt that's holding you prisoner? What would you say to your internal critic?

As you read through this book, we are going to work on this vision until it becomes a solid roadmap that will get you to take action and stop being scared.

For some, writing is a business and they approach it as such, forming an actual business plan. They may even hold business meetings around it. For others, it's a creative process, and the business aspect comes second. Their mission might have little to do with making money or growing an email list and more to do with spreading a particular message.

When you're ready, I want you to decide what kind of writer you are—business-oriented, creatively focused, or both? You might wonder why this is important. Deciding the goal and purpose of your mission has everything to do with how you face challenges and obstacles.

Right now, begin visualizing your lifestyle as a writer. See how everything looks in six months, one year, and even five years from now.

Then identify the fearful obstacles that are preventing you from reaching this goal. What challenges would you need to overcome to get where you want to be as an author? Why aren't you there now? What is stopping you from beginning your journey? Perhaps you've already published your book and you're looking to take it to the next level, but something is holding you back.

You are taking a brave leap. According to writer Joseph Epstein, "81% of Americans feel they have a book in them...and should write it." But only one percent ever takes action towards starting a book, and even fewer will finish and go on to make an actual living from their writing.

If I can add to that, only a smaller percentage of that one percent can write, promote, and launch a book the correct way. Just about anyone can write a twenty-thousand word eBook, for example. But when it comes to launching it, they don't do it right. They fail to connect with people, influencers, and even with their own branding.

This results in the author's message being misunderstood and lost. They focus so much on getting the writing finished that they forget about the work that comes after, the connections we have to make and the people who can help us if we have the courage to reach out to them.

Yes, ninety-nine percent of the time, authors fail due to a lack of belief in their mission, perfectionistic tendencies that hold them back, and multiple fears that feed their doubts.

Identifying Yourself as a Rejected Author

Rejection as an author is an elusive concept. When you think of rejection, what is the first thing that comes to mind? Perhaps a pile of rejection letters from publishers. Maybe rejection makes you think of negative remarks about you on social media. Maybe someone called you out because something you wrote didn't make sense to them.

Whatever the reason, rejection and the fear of being criticized is very real. Some people handle it well. Others allow the fear of criticism or vulnerability to hold them back from marketing, publishing, or writing altogether.

We tend not to think beyond the rejection letter. If you're a self-published author who has no intention of submitting to a traditional publisher, you might be tricked into thinking rejection doesn't exist and that you can publish your book without making noise.

But if you really want to make it, this is where the rubber meets the road, when the people who go the distance break their fears of writing and publishing and develop the right mindset that puts their work in the hands of those who need it most.

Instead of fearing traditional publishers, we fear the reactions of our fans and critics. We fear those who can give us instant feedback with brutal honesty. We often hear about big-name authors such as Stephen King or J.K. Rowling whose works were rejected many times over before being accepted. You might be thinking, "But that's different. They have talent and great stories. Sure, they were rejected in the beginning, but now?"

Everyone starts at the same place. It begins with an idea, a first sentence, and completing that first page. I don't know of anyone who was an instant success. Regardless if you are a Hemingway or Fitzgerald, the finished works they completed went through multiple drafts. What we see as perfection is really a lifetime of dedication to practicing a craft. It takes perseverance and persistence, two essential traits we will examine in detail later on in the book.

You can have all the talent in the world, but without the backbone of persistence, perseverance and passion to push yourself to the finish line, it won't matter. I believe these two traits beat out raw talent in the end.

Stephen King, still one of today's most popular fiction writers since his launch of *Carrie* in 1974, has loads of talent and is obviously gifted in storytelling. But he also works hard by writing consistently and persevering. He has said he writes six pages a day, averaging two thousand words per day. His success wasn't an overnight success, and yours won't be either. You might say he got lucky, but long-term "luck" is simply the determination to move forward no matter what happens.

Your fears can be lessened when you commit to moving toward where you want to be.

The next question is this: What rejection have you experienced in the past, and how did you handle it?

Think about this for a few minutes. Grab some coffee and ponder the events that took place. How you dealt with your fear of rejection in the past is how you'll deal with it now as a writer.

If you are in the habit of running when things go wrong, you may want to run when you get a bad review or when someone says something negative about your writing. It's important to remember that everyone will receive your message differently regardless of whether you're writing fiction or nonfiction.

As writers and creative people, our mission is to publish content that entertains or instructs; it won't resonate with everyone. How you handle your rejection now is probably how you'll deal with it in all areas of your life. Will you shrug it off and keep going? Or will you give up in frustration, and believe the worst about your writing?

There are a lot of authors who make a killing on their work, but they aren't necessarily "great writers." Not everybody will like your work, but you don't have to please everyone. You only need to target your ideal reader—the one person you're trying to reach with your story or lesson.

This book has three objectives:

1. Provide you with basic strategies to plow through your fears, doubt, and anxieties so that you can write like a pro.
2. Give you the tools to take action and market yourself with confidence to the people who need what you have to share.
3. Turn your dreams of being a successful author into a reality as you write book after book.

Here's how I can help you:

I am a *rejection free confidence coach* and personal development leader. I have also written over thirty books and worked through many of the tough spots writers deal with. I help people create their work, break through the barriers holding them back, and launch their dreams. I have coached over two thousand writers to help them launch their books. A huge part of this involved working through the fear of criticism and the self-doubt people carry.

I have mastered the art of living in fear; now, I work toward mastering the art of freedom. I have written several books on rejection and I teach people how to better their lives through constant self-improvement. You won't live forever, so why not live for today and do what you love.

This is the only way we can achieve our goals and live our dreams. If you stay where you are and do what you've always done, you'll be in the same spot twenty years from now. Don't leave yourself wondering, "If only I had..."

It doesn't matter whether you write nonfiction or fiction, a blog, or ghostwrite, dealing with rejection is a natural enemy. Plagued with uncertainty and doubt, we are faced with a future that seems bleak. Will I finish this book? Can I finish it? Am I hopeless? What was I thinking when I started writing? Am I insane?

It can be a lonely path to follow. That is why I wrote this book. Think of it as a companion on the road to writing and publishing your book. Even if you're scared, you can do this. You can do it scared.

Writing is hard work, but before we begin writing, we're told we have to be social and market our work on top of everything else. Does this mean we have to make short videos and post to YouTube every week? Should we post to a private Facebook group? I already have a Facebook account. Why would I want another one?

The dilemma goes on. There is so much to think about that authors get bogged down in action paralysis. With too much to do, we end up doing nothing.

And the guilt moves in. The critic comes to life. The page remains blank, the cursor blinking. You tell yourself that maybe this isn't for you. Self-doubt throws in two cents and tells you to go back to your other job because you can't possibly succeed at this one.

This book won't teach you how to write. Instead, this book deals with the topic that most are afraid to discuss: the fear of writing and how to get past it so you can publish your book.

By the time you are halfway through *Rejection Free for Authors*, you'll be itching to get your writing on track. But even better, you'll be less fearful of the process and you will be armed with solid strategies on dealing with rejection and uncertainty.

I am going to share with you the techniques and action plan I use when coaching authors through the difficulties of writing, editing, publishing, and marketing.

Ready?

Let's go.

Now is the Time to Defeat Your Fears

"After rejection – misery, then thoughts of revenge, and finally, oh well, another try elsewhere."

— Mason Cooley

I know a lot about rejection. In fact, I had such a bad case of it that I wrote a book about it as part of my recovery process. But getting rejected is part of life, isn't it? Not everything we do is going to be successful or accepted by our friends, family, and peers.

We are rejected for job interviews, pay raises, and yes, people we don't get along with, for whatever reasons, reject us. Rejection doesn't always suck; it's just a part of the process we have to go through before we get to that big YES.

But what about rejection as an author?

Dealing with rejection is part of the process as a writer. The fear of failure is the biggest obstacle that stops most people from starting or finishing their work. Regardless of whether you're on your first, second, or even tenth published book, knowing that your work is out there means it will be judged by readers.

As you deal with your fears, you might have massive self-doubt and ask yourself these or similar questions:

- What if nobody likes my stuff?

- What if my first book doesn't sell?

- What if I get a bad review?

- What if they hate what I write?

- What if I hate what I write?

- What if I don't finish it?

- What if I get criticized for something I wrote?

Fear of publishing a book and seeing it flop is the reason I procrastinated for years. I also wanted to be a good writer and the fear of finding out I couldn't write kept me stuck for a long time. Other fears were about being an average writer, or someone that just ripped off the ideas of other authors and being called out for it. The fear of not being original has always been an obstacle. You may have similar thoughts holding you back.

There are a number of excuses that keep us from moving forward.

Fear stops you from writing your book. If you believe in fear of rejection more than you believe in your dream of being a published author—if you give fear that much power—you might save yourself the humiliation of writing a failed novel that nobody wants, but you'll also miss an incredible journey.

The second thing that's worse than rejection is never giving yourself the chance to be rejected. How can you be rejected from a job interview if you never send in an application? How can you be rejected by a date if you never ask someone out for coffee? How can you be turned away if you never ask for what you want in the first place?

Maybe you already wrote your book and you're weeks or days away from hitting publish. Having second thoughts? Questioning your sanity? Terrified of what readers will think?

I have these fears every time I write a new book, a blog post, or anything that another human being is going to read. To remedy this, I tell myself that the work I've created is meant to either help someone or, entertain him or her. In the end, people will read what they want and formulate whatever opinions they want. As a writer, I did my part by getting the message out there. I write it and then let go of the outcome.

Consider this: A book written that doesn't sell is still a book written. There is a lot of potential for a book to work for you that goes beyond sales and publishing success. At the very least, you can cross it off your bucket list knowing you gave it your best shot and that you're a published author. You can write another book now that you know how.

Consider these writers whose books were once rejected:

Harry Potter and the Sorcerer's Stone by J.K. Rowling was rejected over ten times. One publisher told her, "You'll never get published. People just aren't interested in reading about wizards anymore." I guess he was wrong. Harry Potter was picked up after an agent's daughter nagged him into finding a home for the book.

L. Frank Baum, who wrote *The Wizard of Oz*, was rejected so many times that he kept a journal called "A Record of Failure," a collection of all the rejection letters he received. Somebody thought this book was worth it because *The Wizard of Oz* has since been translated into many languages and adapted into films, musicals, and TV shows.

Stephen King wrote *Carrie*, but before it was published, it was rejected about thirty times. King's wife rescued it from the trash bin where King had "misplaced" it. One rejection letter said, "We are not interested in science fiction which deals with negative utopias. They do not sell." They were wrong, too, because *Carrie* sold one million paperback copies in the first year after its release.

Jack London, rather like Stephen King, kept his rejection letters impaled on a spindle-like device. The impaled letters eventually reached a height of nearly four feet.

Jack Canfield and Mark Victor Hansen, authors of *Chicken Soup for the Soul*, received 134 rejections. The series now has over 200 titles with over 500 million copies sold.

John Grisham's first novel, *A Time To Kill*, was rejected twenty-five times. John Grisham actually self-published the book himself before it was traditionally published. He had 20,000 copies of this book sitting in his garage rotting away.

You Are a Pro

Writing a book can be a long and arduous task. There are many pieces of the process that have to work together. As you write your book, you will have days when it feels like everything is flowing well.

On other days, it feels as if you're fooling yourself. These are the days when we are tested. Will we shelve our unfinished books and take a break, or will we give up completely?

I've seen it happen. There are many could-have-been-authors out there who had good intentions but burned out within a couple of months.

What's the difference between those who make it and those who don't?

The answer is, I don't really know. Some days it is like a race. You start out strong and fizzle out halfway. Some runners start slow and speed up toward the end. Another runner will pace himself, take periodic breaks and get back into it when he's juiced up again. But they all have one thing in common. They want to finish the race. They want to cross the line and it doesn't always matter who is first.

What matters is that you finish. It might take longer than you expected, but as long as you finish the race and don't give up just before the finish line, it doesn't matter how you do it.

I wrote this book because I know you're a writer. If you made it to the end of this book, you can make it to the end of your own book. You'll be tested and there will be days when you think writing isn't for you. But if you started the race, you didn't just end up here by accident.

People don't read books on writing because they are looking for something to do. You came here with a purpose. A message to share with the world. If you don't finish the race, we will never know what your story is.

Get ready for the thrill of writing a book. This is your time. This is for you. Push through the tough moments. When you can't push anymore, ask for help. You don't have to do this alone.

Rejection is the Way to Succeed

Rejection is the natural course to success. You might think, "My book will suck," or "Nobody is going to read what I have to say." Well, your book might not hit the New York Times bestsellers list, but the only thing worse than a bad book is a book that never gets written.

At least give your writing a chance to fail. If it gets rejected, or someone simply says, "I didn't like it," so be it. That is the price you pay for taking a chance on your dream. Keep on writing. You'll get better at it. The first three books you write might go nowhere. You keep writing and your fourth book could be the gem that launches your author dream.

Dan Brown, the international bestselling author of *The Da Vinci Code* and *Lost Symbol*, quit teaching in 1996 to write full time. He published three books from 1998 to 2001 — Digital Fortress, Angels & Demons, and Deception Point — but these first three novels had little success. They each sold less than 10,000 copies in their first printing.

But Dan Brown kept going.

In 2003 The Da Vinci Code, Dan Brown's fourth book, made it to the *New York Times* Bestseller List in the first week of publication. It was also rejected as a novel that was "so badly written." For a book that was so bad, to this day it has sold about 81 million copies and earned Dan Brown about $250 million dollars.

The rejection is always worth it.

As we will see throughout this book, it isn't the rejection that is the problem. Consider this to be the natural path to success, and you will make it through anything. It is how we handle it.

So, commit to writing your book.

Get it out there.

Let the world decide its fate.

The Dream to
Write a Book

"If there's a book that you want to read, but it hasn't been written yet, then you must write it."

— Toni Morrison

When I was growing up, I had a lot of dreams. Like most kids, I wanted those dreams to come true.

My dream was to be a writer. I read all the time, and one of my favorite authors was Stephen King. I remember reading *Christine* in a weekend, and when I started to feel really inspired, I wrote my first book when I was fourteen. I didn't have a typewriter so it was written on legal pads that my father brought home from his office. The paper still had the company logo at the top.

Over the course of eight months, I wrote a science fiction novel that was at least 50,000 words long. I had over four hundred pages hand-written. I was determined to get it published and was even saving up for a typewriter so I could turn it into real pages. You know, like in the movies when the author types up that last page, stuffs it into a big folder and runs to the post office to deliver it to a big publishing house.

I shelved it for a while and took a break from writing. Eventually I stopped writing completely. Life has a way of intervening and leading you astray if you let it.

Well, I let it.

My break from writing turned into weeks, then months, and years. It was twenty years before I started writing again, and in those twenty years a lot happened. I worked in a lot of jobs that had nothing to do with writing, but it was always at the back of my mind.

Writing a book was always something that I was going to do when I had more time, when I felt inspired again, or when the circumstances were finally in my favor.

Looking back, I was fearful of one thing: Starting.

I let fear guide my path and when that happens, we learn to trust our fearful decisions. Choices made from fear lead us away from our dreams.

If your dream is to be a writer, or if you just want to write a damn book for the sake of writing, it starts here. I'm not promising that you will eliminate the fear you have of writing, creating, or promoting yourself as a writer. You may have a fear of rejection like most people do, only yours is a rejection of self. We reject ourselves more than anyone else does.

Regardless of the obstacles, we can change things. Have you started writing but got stuck? Are you already published but struggling to keep the momentum going? Do you worry whether you'll make it as a writer at all or if you're just wasting your time?

Let's bring the dream to life.

The Big WHY of "Why Write a Book?"

In those early days exploring my writing, I knew I had to write books. It wasn't something I had decided to do; it was a deeper calling that left me with no choice but to pursue this path. Writing was all I ever wanted. I felt compelled by a force that wouldn't let my ideas rest. It was either write, or spend my life doing work I hated. Looking at it this way, there really was no choice.

You might be in a similar position. Making a decision to write can change all that. A focused plan of action coupled with enough resilience can break any challenge.

This brings us to one question: Why?

If you have ever seen the TED talks by Simon Sinek, then you know <u>the power of WHY</u> clarifies your vision. Without a good enough reason, we abandon our projects or we never start them.

If you don't know your WHY, this becomes a whatever. And whatever leads to doing work you hate, while your dream dies and you end up spiritually destitute. Emotionally and mentally, we lose the fight when we give in.

Why do people go to work? To earn money.

Why do we need money? To pay bills.

Why do we pay bills? So we can have a life, eat, and play.

Why does this matter? Because that is what people do, and that is the way I was raised.

The WHY factor brings us to this question:

WHY do you want to write a book?

It is to change lives? Make money? Escape from your boring job? I don't care what your reason is, but it has to be powerful enough to drive you to action. It commits you to diving in and getting it done. If you have always wanted to write a book or a series of books, and you're stuck and can't get motivated, then your WHY—your DRIVE—is enough to charge up your willpower. When your reason is a powerful motivator, you will find a way to begin and get it done.

Right now, let's do a brief exercise. Write down the reason you want to write a book. This should be a compelling reason that you can't ignore. When you have a big enough why, the how will present itself. By knowing the why, it drives our determination to new levels. Knowing why turns a spark into a raging inferno. Knowing why turns a scattered mind into a laser focused force of concentration.

If you are struggling with your own fearful mind of doubt and uncertainty, the WHY can set you free. Your mission becomes clear and every action is directed with greater clarity and purpose.

Now...consider these questions.

- Why is your book important?

- What value are you bringing into people's lives?

- What is the single biggest impact this book will have on your life? Your business? Your family?

- What will happen if you don't write?

- What are the consequences of failing?

The Fear of the Page

Most people are terrified of people reading what they write, as if their words are secret confessions. Well, I may have as many secrets as the next person, but I haven't published any of them yet.

Writing is hard work. The only thing harder is thinking about writing. Putting it off is hard work, too. But if you think about it, you write every day. How often do you fret over grammar or misspelled words? When you write an email, do you worry about grammar, punctuation, or spelling?

Are you afraid the recipient will read it and wonder, "Where did this person go to school?" If you're anything like me, I write it to say what I have to say and send it off.

But now the rules are different.

Now you're writing a book.

Writing suddenly has a deeper purpose. We are writing about something that interests us and we really care about it. We also know if it gets published it will be out there for others to read. They'll talk about it and somebody might even leave a review.

Once you set out to write a book, people take notice. Words can change a life. Influence is a big reason to write your books.

Such a project has a certain stigma attached to it. We place important emphasis on the craft as if it is something sacred and creative that only a select few can take part in.

WHY do you want to write?

WHY will you be up early every morning to get words down on paper?

WHY will you put your reputation on the line?

How do you feel when you think about and visualize your WHY happening for you? Imagine someone asks you to explain the core idea of your book. What would you tell them?

The Formula for Drive

Anyone can write a book. You don't even have to have fully functioning fingers or hands. Stephen Hawking, who has motor neuron disease, writes with a small sensor activated by a muscle in his cheek so that he can type characters and numbers on his keyboard.

Hirotada Ototake, who was born without any limbs, has written the third biggest bestselling book in Japan entitled *No One's Perfect*.

Your drive and perseverance is what you have to tap into and ignite. Forget about talent or learning perfect grammar. That will only get you so far.

Where there is a willingness to create, there is a corresponding action to take. You just have to show up and practice your craft. But Stephen Hawking also has that same drive.

How does drive have anything to do with writing? It's not the same as motivation. When we are feeling unmotivated, we can put things off indefinitely. But to have drive is to be driven by a deeper purpose that overrides all motivation. You don't need motivation or productivity tips when you listen to your drive.

It is the compelling need to write, tell a story, or share your message. It is the WHY in action, and it is the call to action that gets you moving ahead.

You feel this absolute necessity to get your book out there. That's why you are reading this book. The authors I mentioned all have drive. When rejection letters start piling up until we can no longer squeeze them into the kitchen drawer, we know it's our internal drive that pushes us through.

It is a mindset that will not permit giving up, and it's a big part of the success formula whether you're writing one book or ten.

Create Your Own Work

Nothing can give you greater pleasure than working on something that matters to you. When you write, you get to choose the topic. Nobody is handing you a report and saying, "Here, have this done by Tuesday." You are in charge of your own destiny when you can write a story or teach a subject to someone who needs your expertise.

In the end, it's all about adding value to another person's life. You are writing to entertain, provide information or offer a solution to a reader's problem.

Before we continue, consider the answer to this question: What is the WHY for writing your book?

What drives you to create a book that nobody may read? What ambitions are behind your purpose? Do you want to create a second source of income? Are you using the book to fuel your business? Do you want to do public speaking or brand yourself as an authority in a certain niche?

If you write fiction, you have a passion for storytelling. You want to share your story with the world and entertain, thrill, or build an audience.

The WHY is big, and if you do anything today, ask yourself WHY you are writing. What propels you?

Here are some big reasons people have shared with me. I want to write a book so I can:

- Stay at home and work where my family is.

- Travel the world and make a living as an author.

- Become a TED X speaker.

- Build a second income stream.

- Help people set up a business.

- I don't know. I just have a compelling need to write something. (This is good enough.)

Is your **WHY** big enough?

Your why is what will force you through the bad times. When you don't feel like continuing, your WHY will be bigger than your motivation. People with a huge WHY don't wait to be motivated. They work on their craft when motivation has faded and they are running on pure resiliency.

Knowing your why raises the bar on your confidence and attitude. It's a massive pivot that separates those who make it from those who fail. Your why is bigger than you and the book. It is the core value that people will buy into.

Without a big enough why, you'll struggle to get through the first few chapters, let alone the book. You have to have a certain level of drive to complete your book. You should know why you want it, and be clear about the action steps needed.

You have a longing to share your story, your words, and your ideas. There has never been a better time than now. You don't have to wait twenty years like I did.

You can write that first word right now.

The Psychology of Rejection

"We all learn lessons in life. Some stick, some don't. I have always learned more from rejection and failure than from acceptance and success."

— Henry Rollins

Do you ever think about why rejection is so powerful? When was the last time you were rejected, and do you remember why? How did you deal with it at the time? Have you become more cautious since then?

For most people, not just writers, rejection is a big part of life. A person may not be fully aware of it. When we get rejected, it hurts and can leave an unforgettable scar—being excluded by a group of friends, getting turned down for a promotion, or being rejected when you finally get the courage to ask someone out for a date.

Rejection can be a painful experience. If you go through it enough, you could become desensitized to it. On the other hand, you might choose to avoid it at all costs. If this is the case, we spend the rest of our days running, hiding, and avoiding challenges or the possibility of change.

So, what does this have to do with writing a book?

Everything. As an author of ten books, I have written about rejection from my own personal experiences. I have coached people as well as worked with hundreds of authors to help get them to the publishing stage.

As we worked on the book together, the common theme they shared with me was fear of failure and being disliked.

They feared being criticized, and ultimately, feared they would be ashamed or embarrassed at exposing feelings and emotions in a book. It is true that people may not like your book, might criticize the content, or call you a fraud or even worse.

In other words, writers sometimes get rejected for being themselves.

How do we deal with this? We hide from rejection by avoiding the work that would expose us to this fear. We procrastinate in various ways: Editing a book to death, putting off your book launch indefinitely, or talking about writing a book but never getting beyond the first page.

Writing is a creative act. It is a business for many people, but before we think of it as a business, we treat it like a passion project. We attach ourselves to the words and the story. It becomes a part of us.

According to an article in the *Huffington Post by Guy Winch*, the author of *Emotional First Aid*, rejection can feel just as physical as other types of pain. You might get headaches, pains in your chest, or go through depression. Is it any wonder that our fears about writing are focused intently on avoiding rejection?

I gave up writing for twenty years for two reasons:

1. I never believed that I was good enough to be an author.

2. It was easier to dream about writing than to actually write.

For years I told people that *someday* I was going to write a book. I talked a lot but when it came down to starting, I couldn't do it. As soon as my pen hit the paper, I had this fear come over me. Voices of doubt crept in.

I'd lose focus, often on purpose, just to distract myself so I wouldn't have to finish. What if I finished? Would people actually read it? I lived the fantasy of being a writer because I thought it was something I could do in my spare time.

> *"Too many of us are not living our dreams because we are living our fears."* — **Les Brown**

But after years of reflection, the reason I wasn't writing became obvious. It was the same reason I was stuck in the same day job and doing work that I hated: **I was afraid to do something different**. I was terrified of being judged, ridiculed, or told I had no talent. What if I failed? What if the people who instilled self-doubt in me were right? How would I face them?

As long as I could dream of being a writer, the hope was always there, and I could hold on to it. But if the reality of not being able to write suddenly hit me, what then? I had no more illusions. I had a dream and I was afraid to live that dream.

This, in my opinion, is one of the greater definitions of suffering: When you know precisely what you want in life, and yet, you're too afraid to go after it. You hesitate. The uncertainty of not succeeding becomes bigger than the drive to break that fear and succeed no matter what.

Rejection has killed more dreams than we could ever imagine. People turned old and filled with regret. They never took action on their dreams because the fear held them back. They were waiting for a day that, when it arrived, it would be too late. The fear of failure keeps many from writing and publishing.

In order to avoid that pain, we live beneath ourselves.

Bonnie Ware, a palliative nurse, spent years caring for dying people who were in the last stages of their lives. During the final 12 weeks of life they had left, each patient revealed the five regrets they were still holding onto. Of the five regrets, the #1 regret the patients revealed was:

I wish I'd had the courage to live a life true to myself, not the life others expected of me.

You owe it to yourself to bring your dream to life, and if a part of that is to write a book, the best time to start is now. Don't let it be one of the regrets you have in the end.

When you don't believe in yourself, chances are, nobody else will either. You have to get out there again and again, like an aggressive salesman going after a big sell. I know it's easier said than done.

Take a look at the history of authors who've been rejected by agents and publishers. Think about all the great books we wouldn't have read if these authors had given up.

Rejection has always been a struggle for writers. If our work is published, it's revealed to the public for scrutiny, criticism, or praise.

So, how do writers deal with the fear and anxiety that comes with the craft? How do we press on when we know our works will no longer be private, but put to the test in an overcrowded marketplace?

Dealing with rejection is a skill. Regardless of whether you are writing a book or creating a painting, some will like it and some won't. But the creative can take it because they have a passion for their work that supersedes the fear of not producing it.

It is true that rejection is a fearful experience. In a world that is focused on achievement and success, we inwardly crave success but at the same time we are frightened to pursue it. We buy into what is available to us instead of what we really want.

How do you push past the fear others project onto you?

Visualize your own success. See the action steps you are taking right now. Break your own barriers of doubt by going into yourself and finding the genie that awaits you.

Nobody is going to give you confidence. They might encourage and cheer you on, but your battle for greatness is to fight alone, on the inside, where all great wars take place.

Analyzing Rejection:
Who is Rejecting You?

"Everybody walks past a thousand story ideas every day. The good writers are the ones who see five or six of them. Most people don't see any."

— Orson Wells

As writers, we face the reality of being critiqued and judged. But what is it that our readers are criticizing?

Is it our voice?

Writing style?

The message our writing conveys?

The fear of being called out as a fake?

Typos in the book?

We could make a long list of all the ways writers are targeted, but does it really matter? Let the readers say what they want. They have a voice, too. To move beyond the rejection persona and work as an author who writes and publishes books for the masses, we need to get a few facts straight about what rejection is and why we interpret it as a personal attack.

As psychologist Guy Winch has said, "The greatest damage rejection causes is usually self-inflicted. Just when our self-esteem is hurting most, we go and damage it even further."

While others may comment, judge and give opinions, the real damage is coming from within us.

Your self-esteem is under scrutiny by the little voice inside that speaks to you when you're alone. You could be sitting in front of a blank screen right now and those voices might be saying things like:

- "Who are you to write a book?"

- "Nobody is going to read it, you know that, right?"

- "You don't have the credentials to tell that story. What are you thinking?"

- "You were never very good at writing. Why start now?"

- "Come on, stop pretending. Writing is for creative people, and you just aren't that kind of person."

When we believe in the power of our internal critic, it derails our confidence. We start finding excuses why we shouldn't be writing. We justify the reasons that writing isn't for us. This isn't only something that happens to new authors, but veteran authors go through a similar process, even after hitting the New York Times bestsellers list.

A harsh opinion from a reader can bring feelings of self-doubt to the surface of our fears as a writer. A batch of bad reviews could cause some people to quit writing altogether, or cause them to reconsider if writing is really their thing.

Why is rejection such a painful experience?

According to a report published in the *Michigan News* by Ethan Kross and his team, people experience physical pain when asked to recall a period of rejection. This was discovered when brain scans were analyzed via MRI to see how people reacted when they were asked to consider these parts of their past.

They discovered that there is a definite neural overlap between the intense feelings of social rejection and physical sensations of pain in the body. For example, if you were to be scalded by hot coffee, the resulting pain would be equivalent to looking at a picture of someone who rejected you.

Now, this may seem extreme, but going through rejection as a creative will either toughen people up to push forward, or it will cause them to shrink back in fear and abandon any such notions of being a writer.

Remember this: critical expression is a necessary element for a writer to grow. I know it is tempting to want to please everyone, to write the right thing every time, and to be the writer adored by millions. But a writer has a voice that will be heard by many and scorned by some.

Critics help you grow. This is true if it is your editor, a fan or a best friend reading your book for the first time. Think of criticism as the road to progress. My books would have been poorly written if I hadn't taken the advice of everyone who provided feedback on the content.

Honest feedback can only enhance your work and make it better. The better your writing quality, the more people will enjoy it in the end, and the more books you will sell. Handling criticism can only be overcome by getting as much of it as possible.

Let it move through you and let it hurt if it must. You will adapt and grow a thicker skin. When this happens, you will find out what it means to be a writer. All great creatives will learn to empower their craft so that it rises above the fear of failing.

You can only fail one way: When you give up.

Rejection and Opioids

When you feel physical or emotional pain, your body releases a chemical called opioids. This is our natural painkiller that reduces the impact of the pain. According to research, this is now true of people who go through the pain of rejection, such as a breakup, or the pain of a social rejection.

Now, to take this even further, an individual who releases large amounts of opioids will be better equipped to handle the setbacks of rejection. If someone releases fewer opioids, they could fall victim to rejection easier and be damaged more severely by the aftereffects.

For example, they may give up on something even if they feel passionate about it, just to escape the pain of being criticized. Someone who has a high tolerance for rejection could also be releasing more opioids that enable him or her to better handle emotional pain.

If you're like most creative people, it could mean the difference between succeeding at what you love no matter what, or giving up because the self-doubt, internal criticism, and uncertainty was too much.

But what is the one factor that drives people to thrive while others shrink away?

It is called resilience. This is a powerful personality trait that can determine the amount of pain you can process and handle. If you have weak resilience, you may find it easy to give up and make excuses as to why you can't do something. But with a strong enough will and determination, you can get through any rejection.

Agatha Christie waited four years to get her book published. The famed inventor Thomas Edison had a massive amount of resilience to keep moving ahead when most would have surrendered. Behind all the rejection slips, the years of writing in solitude, and the push to get their material accepted, the authors we have come to know and admire all had resiliency. They wouldn't have made it otherwise.

If you are feeling overwhelmed with the writing process, remember that accomplishing your goal has less to do with talent and more to do with your ability to stick with your plan to finish your book. It's about putting your message out there so that your readers can benefit and learn from what you have to share. Be resilient not just for yourself, but for those who need your book.

Think about the potentially thousands of people who may need a book tonight like the one you are writing. If it is a children's book, this may be the book that a parent needs today to put their children to sleep.

If it is a book on building confidence, your book might have strategies someone can use. If you are writing a book on entrepreneurship, your book could help an aspiring entrepreneur start their online business.

If you're lacking resilience, it is a muscle you can build up. If you are lacking courage, you can find that place of courage within. If you are lacking writing skills or talent, you can practice writing every day to get better at it.

Throughout this book, we will target the elements of fear that a writer experiences. We will look closely at the obstacles that get in our way, and the persistent resilience of authors who make it and those who don't. There are effective strategies you can implement to help you break the fear of the blank page.

If rejection is a painful experience for you, you're not the only one. What matters is how you react to it. Will you let it defeat you, or will you use it as leverage to take action?

The 7 Benefits of Learning to Handle Rejection

"Every time I thought I was being rejected from something good, I was actually being re-directed to something better."

— Steve Maraboli

The fear of rejection, criticism, or harsh judgment is not for authors only. We all have a level of sensitivity when it comes to the challenge of facing any rejection. Life just works that way. But what matters most isn't why you get rejected, but how you deal with it.

How we handle this can have a major impact on our success. If a critical review kills your confidence, take a minute to think about how you can handle the critics and naysayers when they trash your best work.

Most of us don't handle rejection well. We paint the rejection in negative light. We blame ourselves for not being good enough. Instead of having the courage to ask for what we desire, we retreat and avoid the opportunity to get rejected. Instead of plowing through and going for the gold, we accept our failure as the end of the road.

But rejection is just the beginning of the journey. Success is, after all, the avocation of determination. Expect to fail, and fail often.

I found that even after writing numerous books I struggled with the critics and the fear of being judged. But the more I pushed forward, the tougher my mindset became. This is what you can do, too. Your mindset is at the center of your author success. It can make you or break you.

Let's discuss some benefits that are extremely empowering, and why you should make every effort to overcome your rejection issues.

Benefit #1: Defeating Rejection Builds Character

We grow and become stronger when we face the circumstances that scare us. Win or lose, taking a stand when your mind is full of fear and you can't imagine moving forward, but you do anyway, is extremely empowering. You will only know what you are capable of achieving when you decide that you are going to take action and do it anyway.

It is when we can overcome our difficulties that we become better at what we do. The musician plays better when he or she overcomes the adversity of playing a difficult piece. The acrobat performs better when they traverse their fears of a difficult jump. The author writes better when they push aside the feelings of uncertainty lying just below the surface. Building character is the result of years of digging in and not giving up when times are challenging.

Benefit #2: Defeating Rejection Increases Confidence

Confidence comes with forward motion. Passivity keeps you scared. The more you accomplish, the more your confidence grows. Can you imagine writing a book and then reaching out for an endorsement from a well-known author?

When you believe in the craft you are creating, this is what is possible. You can make it happen when you are more confident. Confidence isn't just a feeling, it is a state of mind. You don't have to be confident before taking action.

Confidence is the result of taking action when you are scared. First, you do what terrifies you the most, then you build on your confidence later.

Benefit #3: Increases Your Passion to Create More

Success builds success, and taking action creates the need for more action to be taken. When you stand against the resistance that keeps you scared, you tap into your creative passion. You will fall in love with your craft no matter what they say.

If we try to create what others want, it doesn't lend to our purpose and we end up doing it to please the masses. You can only create work you love when it comes from a place of passion. This can be the passion we feel in trying to help other people. It can come from knowing we are doing the work we were born to do.

Benefit #4: Increases Your Earning Power

Do you imagine yourself selling hundreds of books a day? How about thousands? When you can defeat your fears of rejection, you increase the chances of earning more. People who give up before they make it rarely make enough money to pay for their first book production. The more you persevere, the more you will boost your potential to earn money doing what you love.

It is one thing to spend your life doing something you love; but it is another to do what you love and get paid well for it. I know writers who are traveling the world living from a beach and earning money doing what they love to do: Write and travel.

Another writer is spending more time at home now with her family, earning a full time income. She has more time now for her children because she sets her own schedule and isn't relying on a corporate job to pay the bills while at the mercy of a fixed time schedule.

Benefit #5: Offers Credibility to Your Success Story

Successful authors pushed through all the rejection letters. Many were told their work was no good or that it was unfit for publication. We are raised to believe that rejection is the same as failure.

Rejection is the necessary path to achieving what you want. Push through the naysayers, and one day, when you arrive at the point in which you are completely satisfied with your success, you will have your own story to tell.

Keep telling your story of how you were once one of those writers who dreamed of making it. Build your story as you experience life each day working on a dream to make a difference, tell a story, and share your voice. Turn your struggle into a success story that inspires others.

Benefit #6: Increases Your Resilience

Action begets action. The more forward momentum you produce, the stronger your resolve. You become unstoppable. By making a decision to handle whatever rejection comes your way, you are choosing to become desensitized to fear. Uncertainty and doubt stand no chance when it comes to the resilient mind.

Resilience makes you able to handle challenges that many run from. You become stronger with criticism and the chance of being rejected at any time. Best of all, you welcome it because it gives you the chance to grow.

Benefit #7: Rejection Leads to Something Better

There are times when it seems like rejection is all there is. You are being rejected by either someone else or yourself. This is when we have choices to make. You can give up and do something else or keep pushing forward hoping you get a breakthrough.

While rejection can be a frustrating experience, it's like riding waves. Keep your bow pointed toward your destination and you could end up on the other side, in a place you never would have reached if you had turned around.

This is known as a rejection redirect, when you direct the power of the rejection toward something better. This takes a certain mindset that puts you on a different stage. Stick with it enough and you'll get used to the fear of rejection. Soon, it won't be a fear anymore; it will be the motivating factor that pushes you ahead.

"Who wants to become a writer? And why? Because it's the answer to everything.... It's the streaming reason for living. To note, to pin down, to build up, to create, to be astonished at nothing, to cherish the oddities, to let nothing go down the drain, to make something, to make a great flower out of life, even if it's a cactus."

— Enid Bagnold

The 5 Traits of Successful Authors

"We're past the age of heroes and hero kings. ... Most of our lives are basically mundane and dull, and it's up to the writer to find ways to make them interesting."

— John Updike

You might think rejection only happens to you, and that everyone else is an instant success. After all, when we hear names like Grisham, King, and Dr. Seuss, it's hard to imagine they were ever unsuccessful.

They experienced rejection, too. It's part of the game, and it is a big part of living the journey. But it doesn't matter that their work was rejected early on; what matters is what they did about it.

We know what it means to fail and the consequences involved, so we try to avoid failure.

But when it comes to writing, our rejection is an internal sense of failure. When you write a book, you are speaking to a particular audience. They have bought into your story and are investing their time in reading your book. We fear we might let them down. But even worse than that, it's about letting ourselves down.

If your dream is to be a writer, and you struggle to write well, the material won't be very good in the beginning. It won't be like *Watership Down* or Frank Herbert's *Dune*.

We have to accept that the business we have chosen can be a rough road to traverse when criticism is par for the course.

Writers need tough skin, tougher than most, because in the end it's those who work through the resistance that end up with the bestsellers.

But don't let this discourage you. You don't have to sell your house and hole up in a secluded cabin in the middle of the forest to call yourself a writer. You don't have to make a million dollars a year, either, to be considered successful.

Regardless of how much money you make—or how little—you have something you want to write or a story that needs to be told.

Let's take a look at some of the world's most prolific and successful authors. These writers were rejected more than once before setting out on their publishing careers.

This gives us a realistic vision of what it is like to be a struggling writer. Regardless of whether you are traditionally published or self-published, facing criticism and rejection is part of the game plan. Trying to avoid it by buying into perfection or stalling the publishing process because you think your work isn't good enough is an escape tactic to avoid being rejected. There is a mantra that I live by that has forced my writing into a hardline funnel:

Fail fast and fail often.

This means you should not tread lightly. Push forward at lightning speed, instead. Take massive action and fail as many times as you can.

We try to avoid the pitfalls by tiptoeing around what could be a mistake. In the end, we either don't finish our work, or we launch a book so quietly that we avoid attention to the point that it doesn't go anywhere.

"You fail only if you stop writing." **— Ray Bradbury**

Great writers fail. Good writers fail. Bad writers still publish books and fail. Writers who aspire to publish but never do fail the most because nobody gets to read their work.

Let's take a look at the names of some authors who pushed through the pain to get published. Perseverance and the patience to keep pushing forward pays off. The redeeming quality of successful authors isn't how well they write, but how well they maneuver through the pitfalls and hard work that lies ahead.

The difficult road is **worth the risk**.

Anne Frank's *The Diary of a Young Girl* was rejected fifteen times before it was published.

Stephen King's *Carrie* was rejected thirty times before it was published.

William Golding's *The Lord of the Flies* was rejected twenty times before it was published.

Margaret Mitchell's *Gone with the Wind* was rejected thirty-eight times before it was published.

John le Carré's *The Spy Who Came in from the Cold* was passed on because le Carré "hasn't got any future."

Frank Herbert's *Dune* was rejected twenty-three times before it was published.

J.K. Rowling's *Harry Potter and the Sorcerer's Stone* was rejected twelve times and J.K. Rowling was told, "Don't quit your day job."

Agatha Christie had to wait four years before getting published.

George Orwell's *Animal Farm* was rejected because "there is no market for animal stories in the USA."

John Grisham's *A Time to Kill* was rejected by sixteen publishers before Grisham found an agent who eventually rejected him, as well.

Alex Haley, author of *Roots*, wrote every day for eight years before finding success.

Robert M. Persig's *Zen and the Art of Motorcycle Maintenance* was rejected 121 times before it was published.

William Faulkner's *Sanctuary* was called "unpublishable."

Sydney Sheldon's *The Naked Face* was turned down by five publishers. It was finally sold to William Morrow for $1,000 and published in 1970. Sheldon, who hadn't started writing until he was fifty, sold over three hundred million copies worldwide.

Chicken Soup for the Soul by **Jack Canfield and Mark Hanson** was rejected 140 times and the authors told, "Anthologies don't sell." Now, the book that launched a successful franchise has sold 125 million copies.

Why should we hide from the world when so many authors faced that fear and pushed through to success? What makes us any different? Your story matters. Your craft matters. Somebody out there needs your book and your message.

By holding on to the fear, you are holding back on something your fans need. If you have the solution to a problem that would make someone else's life better, wouldn't you want to share it? I know I would. If you are a fiction writer and your story could add value to people's lives, don't you want to share it with as many as possible?

The time has come to stop rejecting yourself. Stop rejecting the author and start to reject the rejection. This is how we begin to heal. This is how we can finish writing a book. This is how our work will reach hungry fans who need to hear our story. Your book might have the potential to change a life, but you'll never know the course of that impact if you stay stuck.

The 5 Traits of Rejected Authors

Now that we have looked at a short list of some of the most profound rejected authors, what is it that pushed them to succeed? How can we, as aspiring writers, learn from these lessons?

1. Writing is a long-term game.

Agatha Christie persevered for four years before she was accepted. While some may be rejected a handful of times, others can be rejected hundreds of times. The writer could end up thinking their work isn't any good and simply give up.

For a self-published author, it's different. Anyone can write and publish a book. It might get rejected by readers if they really hate it, but you won't be waiting for that rejection letter. However, it doesn't mean rejection isn't still a part of the process.

To succeed, we have to write for the long-term and adjust to the changes in trends and technology. We have to be marketers and salespeople as well. We are not just wearing the hats of content creators, but we become the driving force behind the success of our own work.

2. Deal with insecurity, sensitivity, and sense of vulnerability.

By nature, many writers are introverts. The stereotype of a writer sitting alone in a cabin somewhere, crafting his or her novel, is a thing of the past. You can still do that, but when the book is done, it's time to come out of your shell and get moving on pushing the book into the world. This brings up a lot of fears. The fear of critics not liking it, the fear of being criticized on social media, or the fear of shooting a five-minute video as an introduction to your book.

As writers, we have to push through vulnerability. It may be scary, but doing it scared is the only way to get used to promoting your material.

Are you feeling insecure because you might be judged?

Are you insecure because you have never believed in yourself?

Are you feeling vulnerable because people might see something you don't want them to see?

It can be scary stuff. But the other option is to pack up and go home. If you are here to kill the inner rejection, it begins with facing the thoughts and fears that scare you.

3. Believe in your work.

Believing in yourself is important for any writer. Aside from having an unbroken resilience to making their books work, authors who make it are totally dedicated to getting their writing published.

Writers who self-publish must launch, promote, market, and sell their own book. The book will never see the inside of a bookstore unless the author sells enough to attract a traditional publisher, or is able to get their book connected to a distributor that works with bookstores.

Our goal here is to toughen up your skin so that you can do what writers do best. But if we fail to deal with our confidence, the rest won't matter. If we are terrified of rejection, it can hold us back from taking the action needed to see the book through to the end.

To finish your book, you have to believe in it completely. If you don't, the readers won't. Show them how passionate you are about your work, and you won't have to worry about selling anything. The book will sell itself.

When you **believe**, you **achieve**.

4. Rejected authors don't give up.

You knew this one was coming. If there is anything that works best for really making it as a successful author, it is this: Stick to it. Don't give up. If your book gets rejected, take whatever feedback you get and go with it. But ask yourself why it was rejected. Is there something in the book that needs to be fixed?

Next, get more than one opinion. Did you get a negative review? A lot of authors—especially self-published authors—get really worked up over one negative review. It happens. Was the review valid or was the reader just in a bad mood? How many negative reviews do you have compared to positive? When you get a bad review, learn from it and move on. Stick with it. Keep charging forward.

Take a day off writing if you want. In fact, I would recommend working five days a week and taking two off. Aside from that, stick to your writing schedule.

Stick with your plan. Stick with your book until it is edited. Stick with it to the publishing stage. Stick with it when readers reject it.

Then, move on to the next project.

5. Writers write.

Writing is a long-term game and, as Jeff Goins said, you should have a plan to create a lot of material consistently over the long-term. Later, I will cover practical strategies for getting your writing done even if you can't type very well.

By sticking to a regular writing schedule, you will be able to get your draft done within sixty days or less, depending on length and topic. This book doesn't go into the details of writing a draft, but if you are looking for something to help you get started, you can check these out:

Lifelong Writing Habit: *The Secret to Writing Every Day: Write Faster, Write Smarter* by Chris Fox

On Writing Well: *The Classic Guide to Writing Nonfiction* by William Zinsser

How to Write a Nonfiction eBook in 21 Days - *That Readers LOVE!* By Steve Scott

Many writers talk about how hard writing is. While it is a lot of work, the real battle is with ourselves.

Our insecurities try to convince us that we're not good enough, and that if we'd be more realistic we would have less fear about carrying out seemingly impossible tasks.

You are here to write and build something with your voice and craft. Don't hold back and don't let yourself get in the way of your own success.

We can stand up to the pain of rejection. Let's cover the basic fundamentals of rejection, and how we can win in the face of our own self-doubt and uncertainty.

Leverage Rejection to Your Advantage

"By the time I was fourteen the nail in my wall would no longer support the weight of the rejection slips impaled upon it. I replaced the nail with a spike and went on writing."

— Stephen King

We discussed how writers might avoid rejection. Now let's look at it from another angle that empowers our writing and strengthens our position as authors. While rejection isn't a pleasant experience to go through, you can reverse your mindset to deal with rejection differently.

Here's a brief quote from **Joanna Penn's** book, *The Successful Author Mindset*:

"Build up resilience and a thicker skin over time, because, as a creative, you will face criticism and rejection throughout your whole career. You're never going to please everyone, so be aware that if you put your work into the world, there will be comments you don't like."

Rejection isn't a bad thing. Painful, yes, and uncomfortable to go through, but behind the veil of critics and people saying "no thanks" in a not-so-polite manner, we can learn to desensitize our fragility, build up a tougher skin, and keep writing. You can observe how you're thinking and feeling about yourself in the moment as you experience rejection.

Let's think about this for a minute. Close your eyes and visualize a time in which you were going through rejection. Was it in a relationship? Were you turned down by someone you were interested in? Now, did you give up on relationships altogether, or did you keep trying? Chances are, you had a date eventually because you took a chance on someone and they took a chance on you.

Rejection, for what it's worth, can be redirected toward something better—but only if we continue pushing forward as our best selves when the world is telling us to stop.

Now, let's look at nine rejections sent to now-famous authors. Today, these writers are considered pioneers in literature. How would you feel if this was said about your work? What approach would you take and how would you react?

1. H.G. Wells: Partial rejection letter for *War of the Worlds*.

> "An endless nightmare. I think the verdict would be, 'Oh don't read that horrid book."

Despite this editor's opinion, the story about an alien invasion is still in print nearly 120 years later.

2. D.H. Lawrence: A publisher's advice to Lawrence after reading *Lady Chatterley's Lover*.

> "For your own sake please don't publish this book."

3. John Updike: Rejection letter for *Rabbit Run* in 1959.

> "Unfortunately we have decided against publishing your manuscript, as we feel it is far too divorced from reality. Not once in the entire novel does a character get the hiccups. This is an extremely common condition that happens to everyone, and yet none of the so-called 'characters' in your work ever suffer from it. Needless to say, we will not be publishing the hiccup-less fantasy novel titled *Rabbit Run* now or any time in the near future."

4. Ernest Hemingway: Rejection letter for *The Sun Also Rises* in 1925.

> "If I may be frank—you certainly are in your prose—I found your efforts to be both tedious and offensive. You really are a man's man, aren't you? I wouldn't be surprised to hear that you had penned this entire story locked up at the club, ink in one hand, brandy in the other. Your bombastic, dipsomaniac, where-to-now characters had me reaching for my own glass of brandy."

The novel was published by Scribner the following year, and went on to become one of Hemingway's most popular publications.

5. Alice Walker: Rejection slip for *The Color Purple* in 1981.

> "While your piece, *The Color Purple*, presents a compelling and thoroughly moving narrative, we were bothered with your decision to end every sentence with an exclamation point. As a reader, this was extremely jarring. I am afraid, for this reason, we are forced to make the difficult decision to pass on your manuscript."

6. J.R.R. Tolkien: Rejection slip for *The Lord of the Rings* in 1953.

> "The majority of your *Lord of the Rings* manuscript is exquisitely realized. However, the story's impact is somewhat undermined by the fact that the entire novel is in quotes that are ultimately attributed to 'some old dumbass in a porta-potty somewhere' on the very last page. Sadly, it's a no for us."

We all know how this series turned out.

7. Ursula K. Le Guin: Rejection letter sent to her agent for *The Left Hand of Darkness* in 1968.

"Ursula K. Le Guin writes extremely well, but I'm sorry to have to say that on the basis of that highly distinguishing quality alone I cannot make you an offer for the novel. The book is so complicated by details of reference and information, the interim legends become so much of a nuisance despite their relevance, that the very action of the story seems to be to become hopelessly bogged down and the book, eventually, unreadable. The whole is so dry and airless, so lacking in pace, that whatever drama the novel might have had is entirely dissipated by, what does seem, a great deal of the time, to be extraneous material."

The Left Hand of Darkness went on to win the 1969 Nebula Award for Best Novel and the 1970 Hugo Award.

8. Vladimir Nabokov: Rejection letter for *Lolita*.

"...overwhelmingly nauseating, even to an enlightened Freudian ... the whole thing is an unsure cross between hideous reality and improbable fantasy. It often becomes a wild neurotic daydream ... I recommend that it be buried under a stone for a thousand years."

Lolita went on to be published in 1955.

9. Louisa May Alcott: Rejection for *Little Women*.

"Stick to teaching."

Alcott dismissed this comment and *Little Women* was published in 1868 and 1869 in two volumes. It is still a popular book today.

Rejection is the cliff from which we all dangle until we decide to let go and be ourselves. Judges, critics, and formulated opinions, as right or wrong as they may be, are like the turbulent waters of the trade.

Now, you may not be in a position in which you would be getting rejection letters, but with today's social media platforms and instant connection to readers, we could be dealing with these types of critics everyday.

We can leverage our experience of rejection by taking three easy steps.

1. Turn the rejection into a challenge.

If you get turned down for a date, you try to get another one. If your company turns you down for a promotion, push harder to get it next time. Whatever the rejection is, you don't have to accept it. You can take it as the first rejection of many. You only need one person to say yes in order to get what you're after.

Make rejection a challenge. This is what Jia Jiang did in his *One Hundred Days to Rejection* challenge. He made it his mission to try to get rejected one hundred times. Some of his attempts were very brazen and almost guaranteed a rejection, but sometimes he was told *yes*.

With writing, it isn't much different. Although the authors who received rejections were not trying to get rejected, it was the rejection that put the drive into their mission. They took each rejection as a learning experience and pushed on.

2. Agree with your critics and deliver a compromise.

Try this strategy. When your work is criticized, agree with them on every point.

"Yes, you're right, that chapter was pretty bad. I'll try to improve it or do a rewrite in the near future."

"I agree, this book wasn't as good as the others I wrote. Maybe you could offer some tips on how to improve it?"

This isn't to say that you really agree with them. You most likely don't at first. But if you take the defensive approach, you are setting yourself up for more of the same and you'll end up in an ongoing argument that will harm your reputation as a professional.

Let people have their say and get on with your day. Your job isn't to be right. Your job is to provide value to people's lives with your writing. Some will like it, some won't. You can't please everyone. Stay fixed on those you can help.

3. Control your response to rejection and criticism.

We can't stop people from voicing an opinion, and why would we want to? If you're being criticized, you are likely doing something right. When I stopped worrying abut pleasing the masses, I started getting reviews from critics who disagreed with my content. That was okay, because I knew someone was reading it.

You can control how you react to a bad review. Will you get angry, or will you instead ponder the comment and take your time to decide whether to reply or leave it alone?

Remember that the discipline to respond with a professional tone says a lot about you as a writer. You are not afraid to tell your story, be bold, be scared, and yet know that someone— even if it's just one person—has benefited from your words and is embracing your message.

Leverage the rejection you fear and turn it into a positive experience. If someone says no, you say yes. If someone tells you that something isn't possible, show him or her the possibilities.

The Excuses Why We Don't Start Writing

"If you're holding out for universal popularity, I'm afraid you will be in this cabin for a very long time."

— J.K. Rowling

You may have read a lot of books in your lifetime and asked yourself, "How does she write like this?"

I can't speak for all writers, but what I do know is that talent is rarely acquired through heredity. What we call natural talent is the result of lots of practice. If you are just starting to write, or even if you have published multiple titles, writing is a talent that improves with practice.

We have to write badly before we write well. Have you ever seen someone sit down at the piano and start playing like Beethoven in the first week? You have to put the time in. You don't even have to be a good writer to write a book. People are not concerned with your creative talent as much as they want you, the author, to provide them with a unique learning experience. Take your readers on a journey and they will follow you.

If you write fiction, your readers want to be entertained with a good story. If you are writing nonfiction, you are creating material to help someone overcome an obstacle or to provide useful information. I've heard many people say, "I don't want my first book to be the worst book I write." While I'd have to agree, this thinking will forever keep you stuck and you'll never even have a first book to talk about.

My first book actually was the worst book I wrote. What did I do? I wrote another book. My second was much better but still not great. What did I do then? I wrote another one. The more I wrote, the better my "natural talent" became. Every book got better. I made changes to my writing style with each new project.

Now, maybe you don't plan to write multiple books and that's fine. But to prepare for your first book, you could spend more time on the rewrite stage. Some authors will painstakingly rewrite paragraph after paragraph. Nothing will ever be perfect, but the more you do it, the better it will get.

Practice your craft until it starts to feel like second nature. You will get better at writing. There are no overnight successes— just people who worked hard at something and refused to give up.

We know it isn't always easy to get to the writing table. We have family obligations, day jobs, and a variety of other tasks that are calling for our attention. But these can also validate our excuses for not writing.

As an author of multiple books and a writing and life coach, I have heard just about every excuse there is for not writing. I've used most of these excuses myself. But an excuse for not writing a book is simply procrastination and struggling against resistance.

We are trying to protect ourselves from embarrassment, only to create a new kind of shame: the shame of not finishing the book we have been talking about for years. We would rather be doing anything other than writing.

Excuses will kill your chances of becoming a published author. There are no good reasons for not writing a book, only good excuses that we convince ourselves are real.

If you really want to be a published author, it is time to get into character and start working. Forget about the bestselling secrets to getting published. The only secret I know is the one that says we have to work hard, stay focused, and check off our daily and weekly goal posts.

Let's take a look at some of these excuses and remove them so that we can get our writing done.

There is no time in my life right now to write.

We are all busy: work, kids, family, community and time spent with friends. Of all the excuses we use to prevent ourselves from writing, this is the one used the most: I have no time. Time is limited for all of us. There are twenty-four hours in a day; this hasn't changed since the beginning of time, and I don't suspect it will. But people around the world every day are accomplishing amazing things with their time.

I used to say I never had the time for writing, but I had enough time to watch two hours of TV every day. I had enough time to surf the net and play games. It occurred to me that if I could write one thousand words an hour and do this for thirty or forty days, I'd be finished the first draft of my book.

You'll find that no matter how busy you are, there is time to write your book. I wrote seven books while raising two young kids and working full-time. I don't think this is an amazing feat. My point is that you can reach your goal as long as you apply yourself.

Later on, we will go over some time management techniques for writing faster. Right now, you can throw this excuse aside. It's no longer valid. You will write your book in the next thirty to sixty days, excuses aside, if you commit to thirty to sixty minutes per day.

Here, let's do the math:

500 words x 60 days = 30,000

1,000 words x 30 days = 30,000

2,000 words x 15 days = 30,000

You may not be a fast typist, but you don't have to be. Pace yourself and set your daily goal. Be realistic. Know how much time you have to commit to writing and apply yourself.

I can't get past my distractions.

We are always surrounded by the danger of being pulled off-course and chasing rabbits into endless fields where we lose our productivity. The hardest part to writing is getting into focus enough to get work done. Writers are always dealing with this, and with today's instant access to endless entertainment and social media, there is no lack of shiny object syndrome pulling us away from the blank page. How can we deal with this effectively?

Here are several tips for handling distraction and getting work done.

Unplug from Wi-Fi.

Turn off your Internet connection. While writing, you don't have to research or look anything up. The moment you do, you leave yourself open to chasing bigger rabbits down the rabbit hole. The Internet is a wonderful thing, but we can get sucked into spending all of our time there and not getting any work done.

During your writing session, you can use software such as Scrivener to work offline. If you come across anything that has to be researched, make a note on the page and get back to it later. This goes for your phone as well. With all the notifications and constant influx of email, staying focused on a single task is a big challenge. Whatever is happening can wait until you have hit your word count for the day. Try leaving your phone in another room so you aren't tempted.

I schedule my Internet time and turn my devices off after eight p.m. This is a hard habit to break in, but it's worth it because it will give you your time back. The time you think you don't have for writing is always there if you cut away at the inessentials.

Try distraction-free writing.

Writing your book is a challenge and there is nothing better than using distraction-free writing software. This is a feature that enables you to write freely without any surrounding noise on your screen. You can find this feature built in to WordPress and Scrivener.

Check out the resources section in this book for direct links to distraction-free software. Remember: focused writers get the work done.

I need more time to perfect my writing.

If I wrote a book called *How to Write the Perfect Book*, I have little doubt it would become a big hit. I know this because in my years of dealing with struggling authors, the desire for perfection is prevalent. It can be the biggest obstacle to getting a book written and published.

Writers are inherently sensitive about the potential of being read by thousands of people. What if they don't like me? What if I suck at writing? How can I deal with bad reviews? Yes, the fear of writing is real, but so is the probability of success if you break through that fear and resistance.

Perfection can really inhibit your writing progress if you let it. When we try to be perfect, it slows down any form of creativity and eventually poisons our enthusiasm. Perfectionists are dreamers who never publish or produce. And when they do, it takes so long to ship their product that they could have written ten books in the time it took to do just one.

Later, I will cover the psychology of the writer who tries to be perfect, and the strategies to overcome this. If this is an area you struggle with, just keep reading.

I compare myself to everyone else.

Most writers, when they believe they failed because they haven't achieved the kind of success they want, experience pain and disappointment. When this happens, we start the comparison game.

When we compare ourselves to bestselling writers who have the success we want, it knocks our self-esteem and confidence right down the ladder. When we compare, we can always find fault in ourselves. *I am not good enough. I'll never reach that level. My life sucks.* For years, I had intense "envy syndrome." I compared myself to writers who were getting the results I wanted. I could feel a combination of resentment and envy.

Everyone is at a different stage in their writing careers.

As a coach, I have heard lots of excuses as to why writers were struggling with completing their books. Some people are too busy. Others worry they don't have the savvy to market their books. They don't have a big enough launch team yet. They are waiting for the perfect moment when everything is in alignment. What is really happening is that they reach a certain point and lose confidence. They are looking for that perfect formula that guarantees success as long as everything is in formation. But it's never perfect.

A book is a convoluted mess until the final stages of production are finished, and that includes editing, formatting, and proofreading.

Make a Decision Now: Are you a writer?

I know what you're thinking: I have never published a book. How can I call myself a writer?

I didn't start to call myself a writer until I had launched my third book, and even then I had doubts. But hiding from your passion isn't going to bring you success.

You could make that decision right now, before you even write a word, or after you've written half the book already. Choose to be the writer you have always wanted to be. Decide that you are writing this book for reasons bigger than yourself. Create your big WHY.

Some believe that to write a book we must write perfect prose. This obstacle gets in the way. We put pressure on ourselves to write as perfectly as possible, and so we write stagnantly, often taking long breaks or trashing the book altogether. As a result, we don't move forward.

We know that a writer is someone who writes. If you want to be a published author, commit to writing at least 500 words a day.

Write in the Moment

To write 500 words in one day probably amounts to about thirty minutes of writing. It isn't a big commitment, so it won't be overwhelming, but it is enough to move you closer to your goal.

During this time, shut out your distractions and focus on the action of fingers to keyboard. This is where the writing happens. You can overcome your fears and doubts when you are writing in the moment.

Implement these action steps:

- Make the time to write. Set up a thirty-minute time block every day. Commit to writing during this time.

- Turn off your distractions, both external and internal.

- Be aware of comparisons to other writers. They worked hard to get where they are, and you will get there, too, if you work just as hard.

- Make the decision to be a writer.

The 7 Reasons
Authors Fail

"One thing that helps is to give myself permission to write badly. I tell myself that I'm going to do my five or 10 pages no matter what, and that I can always tear them up the following morning if I want. I'll have lost nothing—writing and tearing up five pages would leave me no further behind than if I took the day off."

— Lawrence Block

Did you know that out of the eighty-one percent of all people who want to write a book, only one percent ever gets around to doing it? How many of that one percent actually finishes the book? And, for the other eighty percent of could-be authors, what is holding them back?

Here, we'll discuss the seven reasons authors fail. When I say fail, I don't mean failing to become a bestselling author or making a certain amount of money or reaching celebrity status. No, I am talking about the reasons they never get around to actually writing or finishing their book.

Let's discuss each of these and dismantle the framework that's holding you back. But first, the core reasons writers fail are:

Reason to Fail #1: I'm going to write this thing all by myself.

When I first started out, I had a vision of an author as someone who sat in a room by themselves with minimal light, writing until the small hours of the night. This is how I worked for many years. I didn't talk about my writing to anyone, as if the project was a secret.

Then, when I finally finished my book and launched it, I had no following, no friends, and no launch team. I wrote the book myself and I published it myself. Can you guess what happened?

Nothing. I learned that a huge part of succeeding is reaching out to people, connecting, influencing, motivating and adding value. One of the reasons I hesitated was because I feared admitting I was an author. I feared that people would actually read my book.

This fear was the one thing holding me back. Successful people are on the front lines, learning what they need to succeed as authors, sharing and taking both praise and criticism from readers.

If you're isolated and have no support team, your work will likely go nowhere. You need people. You have to connect with them where they're hanging out. This includes social media, forums, and your local area.

Somewhere out there is a group of people looking to read what you are writing. But they won't necessarily come knocking on your door. You need to reach out. Self-publishing a book, if that's your plan, doesn't have to mean doing it by yourself.

Later in this book we will talk about the influencers and people you can find who can help you get where you're going. But you need to show up and let them know you are here and ready for action.

Reason to Fail #2: Until I become successful, I'll just do this as a hobby.

Many authors, when they're first starting out, struggle to take themselves seriously. This is a natural state of mind we develop to protect ourselves from becoming real writers. After all, you might be saying, "Who am I to call myself a writer? I published one book and it didn't sell."

Again, we have the romanticized image of a writer who appears on radio and TV, makes loads of cash, and has to beat their way through the crowds at book signings just to get to the table ahead of the fans.

Writing isn't glamorous for most people. So instead of taking ourselves seriously, we think of it as a hobby that we'll plug away at until something big happens. This mindset has several flaws.

First of all, if writing is just a hobby for you, that's fine. You don't have to read any further into this. But if your true desire is to become a successful author with multiple books and published articles, making money at your craft to support your lifestyle, then a hobby won't cut it. As long as writing is just a "side thing," you'll struggle to meet deadlines for books and fail to make any real money at your craft.

For many years, I told people my hobby was writing. But I wasn't being honest with myself. I knew that my dream was to become a successful full-time author, and it still is. By identifying it as a hobby, I was giving myself permission to stay scared.

By not taking it seriously, I gave priority to other things that ended up wasting time. A hobby is something we do when we feel like it, and when we get around to it. It isn't pressing us for deadlines or to finish a project.

Why wait for success? As long as you identify writing as just a hobby, you'll increase the resistance to write at all. Worst of all, you'll fail to break through and challenge your barriers to becoming a real writer. Until I started to identify my writing as a business, I didn't reach out to influencers to promote my work. I didn't get involved in forums or communities. In other words, I didn't take any of it seriously.

To start building momentum, you should start right now, no matter where you are in the writing process. If you are only half-finished your first novel, get clear about your goals. Are you doing this just for something to do? Do you write to pass the time?

Once again, if this is your hobby, that's great. But if you secretly harbor a powerful desire to grow this into a business, it is time to think of it as one. Your mindset will create the image of your ambition. In other words, what you think and believe you will achieve. You won't become a successful author by accident.

Nobody can discover your work if you are trying to hide it. As a mentor of mine once said to me, "Every great treasure, no matter how well-hidden, has the desire to be found. It doesn't want to be lost forever."

It's up to you to turn from author hobbyist into authorpreneur. A hobbyist is someone who does something purely for passion. But an authorpreneur, although they may be passionate about what they do, seeks to earn an income from their writing.

The scope of this book isn't about how to earn money from writing. However, when you conquer your obstacles, defeat rejection and pursue your writing vigorously, the rest of it will follow. Over time, you'll attract fans and deliver your message to thousands of people.

Reason to Fail #3: I'll work on motivation skills and productivity hacks to keep the momentum going.

Waiting for the motivation to write a book is a strategy built on illusion. For years, I waited for motivation to strike. I wrote when I felt like it. I'd write when I had a good idea and the rest of the time I'd wait for lightning to strike and write when I was in the mood. But writing is like anything else. It takes practice and persistence.

Michael Jordan is one of the best basketball players in the NBA today, but he didn't get that way because he practiced whenever he wanted to. He made a habit of showing up for practice before anyone else and he worked harder than any other player.

Stephen King, who has written over sixty bestselling novels in excess of 300 million copies, writes every day. He doesn't take a day off. This has been his routine for the past forty years. Like it or love it, they are the masters of what they do because they don't rely on motivation or inspiration to make it happen.

The real discipline is mastered on those days when motivation doesn't play a role in getting things done. The motivation comes with practice regardless of how you feel. The days when you don't want to do it are the days you should be doing it.

Many writers get stuck in the editing and revising phase. It's the toughest part of the process. Some people spend years rewriting a book that never sees the light of day. Motivation will not get you to the chair, but having a passion for finishing your project will.

Reason to Fail #4: I'll wait until all the pieces are in place and everything is perfect before getting started.

Attempting to write a perfect manuscript is a major stumbling block for many writers. Perfection is an illusion, but we create it as a necessary element believing that it's responsible for making our work the best it can be.

But there are two sides to striving for perfection. Some authors spend ten or fifteen years writing their books. They agonize over every sentence, writing and rewriting until they're satisfied.

Gone With the Wind took over ten years to write. *The Lord of the Rings Trilogy* took about seventeen years to complete. *Sphere* by Michael Crichton took a whopping twenty years. Although it could take years to write a novel, it can also take mere months.

But it doesn't matter how long it takes you. Many great classics took years to write, but they were still finished and published. You have to start writing your book and worry less about creating perfect prose. Momentum is key. Taking action every day toward completing your book is essential. If you never start, you will never finish.

If you feel as if you're stuck, ask yourself whether you're holding back for fear of something.

Fear of looking stupid?

Being rejected?

Being recognized as an amateur?

Never finishing? (Because you never finish anything.)

Regardless of whether you've written twenty books, or you're on your first book, there is no such thing as the absolute perfect condition for writing. If there were, nothing would ever be published. Begin with a word. A sentence. Write that first page.

The perfectionism we seek is really a fear of starting something new. Once you start, you'll experience ups and downs, mistakes and small failures along the way. These are called learning curves and can only happen if you start with what you have.

Reason to Fail #5: I'll just start and worry about the details later.

While perfection prevents us from getting started, diving in and writing can have its drawbacks, too—even though it's better than doing nothing. Planning your book ahead of time isn't just a wise strategy, but a necessary one. If you don't have a plan and a set of goals, you could keep writing until burnout.

This is an issue that can be easily adjusted with a few hours of strategic planning. This is called outlining. Again, there is nothing wrong with just diving in, but it's best to begin by mapping out your journey so that your motivation, enthusiasm, and energy is put to good use.

Here's what I suggest:

- Set a target date for when your first draft will be finished.

- Set a target date for the publication launch day.

- Mark these dates on a calendar.

- Draft out your book in mind map form.

- Create a basic outline. This doesn't have to be perfect, but spend some time on it. Your outline, if detailed, can shave off hundreds of wasted hours.

- Set up your writing software.

- Set your daily writing time and begin.

You can prepare your work for success by taking a few hours to do some basic planning. The strategy can be fine-tuned and tweaked along the way.

Reason to Fail #6: I'll write this thing, but I won't tell anyone about it.

Similar to writing alone and remaining an introvert, one of the bigger obstacles that people face when it comes to being rejected is shame. It is that deep-down feeling that we just aren't good enough. We hide ourselves behind our craft.

For many years, I wouldn't tell people I was a writer. Not a chance. Not until I made it big time and my books were selling in the millions. But that will never happen realistically. You need to get yourself out there and spread your message. If you don't sell yourself as an author, nobody is going to know you exist.

Here is what you can do to start your personal branding right now.

Set up an author website.

Creating an author website gives your work a professional edge. On your site you can drive traffic to your books and start blogging on the subject matter you're focusing on. A website gives your brand and work a look of authority.

To set up your author website, here is a checklist of action steps to get started:

- **Create a domain name**. This can be your author name or the title of your site. For example, Mark Manson uses markmanson.net and James Patterson uses jamespatterson.com

- Check to see if your domain name is available. You can start with a domain register at Name.com.

- Sign up with a website host. Check out Hostgator or Bluehost.

- Additional sites you can use to build your author site are Squarespace and Wix

- Choose from a free WordPress theme or you can buy professional looking themes at Studiopress themes.

- Have professional author photos taken.

- Set up all of the components for your new site. If you struggle with web design, you could hire reliable freelancers on Fiverr or Upwork.com

Reason to Fail #7: Listening to the internal critic.

We all have that critic inside our head. It's the voice that tells us what we are doing is a waste of time.

You'll never make it. Why even bother, because everyone is so much better at this than you are.

This internal critic is your own mind waging a war on your creative side.

When we believe these messages, we fall down to the criticism. This is the voice that has kept you under for years. It's the voice that rips your story apart and convinces you that watching Netflix is a better option than writing a book.

How do we fight back against this?

Listen to what your own mind is telling you. Pull the fear out of your thoughts. Recognize that it's nothing more than the voice of old fears that have been around for a while. They are scared today because you are taking action.

When we take affirmative steps toward a worthwhile goal, we experience great emotional upset. The fearful side of your mind doesn't want to be challenged. Staying scared is easier, but greatness can never be found there.

One method that works is to keep a list of positive quotes nearby. If you go to war with your internal critic, you need the right weapons to fight back against it. You need to ground yourself in the mindset of a person who truly is a writer. Tell yourself that. Don't let anyone tell you otherwise. The elements of doubt and uncertainty are strong, but they aren't stronger than you.

Giving Yourself Permission to Be an Author

"It's none of their business that you have to learn to write. Let them think you were born that way."

— Ernest Hemingway

When I was writing my first book, I didn't tell anyone about my writing projects. It's as if I was concealing some secret shame that only I knew about. I believed I couldn't be a writer until I had published something, so while writing my first book I kept it under wraps.

But then I published it on Amazon. I didn't tell anyone that I'd published a book. I didn't do anything to launch it, either. Why go through all the trouble of writing a book, paying for editing fees and numerous publishing costs, only to do nothing to market it? The answer was obvious.

I didn't want anyone to read it.

I hadn't given myself permission to be an author.

What if they hated it or wrote a bad review? What if someone mentioned in a Facebook group that my book was crap? I realized that shame was at the core of my creativity. I wanted to be a successful published author, but I was embarrassed to say that I was writing a book. And then to have people read it, comment on it, and criticize it?

I wasn't ready for the rejection I knew would be coming.

So how do authors overcome this fear? You may be past this point of shame or rejection, but let's be honest: even if you've published numerous books, isn't there an underlying hesitation before sending your book to influencers and readers because you're worried they won't like it? Aren't you worried about what they'll think of your creation? Of course you are. You want your message to be heard, not misunderstood.

I used to think writing was about creating the perfect prose and sounding intelligent. I would read books by best-selling authors and copy their style and voice. How could you go wrong if you did what others in your field were trying? The problem with this strategy is that it doesn't sound like you. Your voice comes across like a textbook, or worse, like you are trying to be someone you aren't.

Why copy another person's style?

We fear putting ourselves out there.

People may not like me, but they like this other person, so if I write like him, I'll be more respected. I don't have to tell people I'm doing it, either.

It takes time and practice to discover your own voice, but you can only do this once you accept yourself for who you are. For years, I wanted to be like other authors. I craved and desired their intelligence and the influence they had with readers. They knew what they were talking about and I didn't. They had a certain way with words and could persuade people to take action. Some of them had fancy degrees and doctorates.

What right did I have to write a book? What could I put on the back of my cover that would stand out?

When comparing who I was and what I didn't have to the qualities and backgrounds of those who had so much more, I could only come up with one conclusion: I was less-than. Everything I wrote or crafted had a less-than feeling to it. Why would people read my stuff when they could just as easily pick up someone who is more talented, better qualified or someone who is a best-selling author with thousands of fans?

You can see the dilemma many writers face. We are not just struggling to overcome a lack in confidence, but to aspire to a new level of confidence that we've never had. How do you get readers to buy your work and your brand when you are struggling to believe it yourself?

This comes with knowing your audience. What do they expect from you? Who do you have to be to meet their expectations? You should write your book in the voice that your audience would expect. If you are writing for a medical journal, then writing in a loose tone as if you are hanging out in a coffee shop with a friend may not work very well.

If you are writing a self-help book, the language can be less formal because you are teaching a topic based on your own perspective and not necessarily on something based in scientific research. Fiction writers create a voice for each of the characters, but the overall style of the writer stands out.

Discovering your own voice is as easy as being yourself, but it's also a tough challenge. How can you be yourself if you expect to talk and write like someone else?

Your voice shines through when you are less afraid. Writers don't simply procrastinate because of writer's block or a lack of ideas. They think they don't know how to write. They get caught up in the idea of writing a perfect book. And unless they can convince themselves this can be done, they won't do anything.

We hesitate and put off our writing because we are waiting for influence and permission, as if someone is going to wave a magic wand and we will be transformed into that writer who sits in a cabin in the woods surrounded by inspiration and the sounds of nature.

We come up with all sorts of reasons why it's never the perfect time to write. Here is a list of the best excuses I have used:

- I am not set up in the right creative environment.

- I need to do more research.

- I have to finish reading this book on how to write a book before I can begin.

- There are a hundred things on my to-do list before I can commit to writing this.

- I don't have enough money to publish a book right now.

- There will be time to write after the kids go to college next year.

Most of our excuses revolve around resources—not enough time, money, or talent. But it doesn't cost anything to sit at a keyboard and type. You don't need any special software either. GoogleDocs is free and Word is the standard used across the industry.

Talent comes with practice. The more you write, the better writer you become. When it comes to money, to publish a book, you can still do it for under $1000. This will include the editing, cover and formatting. That is a lot of money but if you find ways to save here and there, you could scrape the cash together. With limited resources, you can still produce a good, quality book.

What is more important than resources is being resourceful. This involves finding a way no matter what to achieve your goal. Resourcefulness is a powerful skill and it is one that you can call on anytime. Be resourceful and you will always find a way.

Write What You Love and Build Author Identity

"Just write every day of your life. Read intensely. Then see what happens. Most of my friends who are put on that diet have very pleasant careers."

— Ray Bradbury

As I mentioned in the first chapter, I refused to call myself a writer for many years. I hid my work from everyone except my closest friends. Even after self-publishing my first book, I didn't tell anyone about it because I was afraid they'd read it and dislike it.

I held some secret shame when it came to writing, as if I feared offending someone. I later learned that it's part of the journey. Our words inspire, educate, and at times, make people angry if they don't like an opinion or idea.

But like a friend of mine once said, "You don't need permission to be a writer. Give yourself permission to become whatever you want. Nobody can question that."

For years, I struggled with defining myself as someone who writes. I told myself and others that it was just a hobby. A writer, after all, is someone like Stephen King or Anthony Robbins who sells millions of copies. Until I could reach that status, I felt determined to keep my writing a dirty little secret. I would start to talk about it only after I achieved a significant victory that could justify calling myself a writer.

But this is a bad strategy. What I was really hiding from was *myself*. Even after I published my third book and it became a bestseller, I was still holding back. I shared this success with people in my small circle, but beyond that, I still tapped into that fear of rejection.

What if I got invited to take part in an interview or podcast? What if I was regarded as an authority on a particular topic and the interviewer discovered I didn't really know that much about it after all?

Fear was in control of my writing career. As long as fear had control, my work would always remain a secret.

Perfection. Fear. Rejection.

These are powerful devices that destroy more creatives than you can imagine. When we wait for perfection before taking action, we never take action. When we live according to fear instead of letting the world see who we are, we ruin our chances of becoming great.

When we fear rejection and stay confined within limitations, we learn to live as mediocre dependents. Our goal is to rip these negative forces from our lives and write with love.

Writing with Love

I broke through my fear of becoming a writer when one of my mentors said, "The reason you are scared is because you're afraid to let the beast go. You think you can contain what is dying to break out. Regardless of whether you write alone and tell nobody, or you write for somebody else, denying what you are is denying the world of something great. So be a writer if you want to be. Be a chef. Be what you want to be and not what anyone else expects."

Author and blogger Jeff Goins related a similar story when a friend of his once said, "*You are a writer.* You just need to *write.*"

Expectations aside, if you write it, readers may come. They might not. But if you give up, nobody will come and you'll always be wondering, "If only I had..."

I started to write with a determined purpose. I was already getting fan mail and comments from people who liked my stuff. This numbed my fear of rejection and I started to believe in my work. If ten people liked what I had to say, who's to say one hundred or even five hundred readers wouldn't enjoy it? I set out with a greater purpose: to write what I love for those who needed it.

When you write with love, it sets your passion free. The love of writing has no restraints and it doesn't judge. You just do it and hope for the best. Love lets you share your message openly. And just like love, some people can accept you and others will reject you. But what matters most is that you accept yourself and keep going.

Perfection is full of fear and it controls our work to the point that we freeze up when faced with uncertainty. When I was focused on perfection, I wasn't writing for anyone but myself. Your readers don't care about perfection. They only care if you're going to entertain them or help them, or both.

Next, I stopped referring to writing as a hobby. It was now my business and I was actually making more money from this than any hobby I ever had. Maybe writing is your hobby while you're working a full-time job, but if your dream is to do this full-time, then it's time to start identifying yourself as a writer. It's scary but get the word out there. When someone asks you what you write, give them a concise answer as if you're selling your services.

When people asked me what I wrote, I would reply, "Oh, you know, just self-help stuff."

This drew a blank look and people would say, "Oh, you mean like that Tony Robbins guy?"

I'd say, "Yeah, Like that."

But it wasn't like that at all. I was still holding back and afraid to tell people what I really did. Just telling people you are writer is one thing but getting clear about the kind of writing you do is essential. There is a huge difference between a car salesman who just sells cars, and a salesman who works for Ferrari and specializes in the high-end market. You need to know exactly what kind of vehicle you are selling and who your client is—or in this case, your audience.

Be clear about the kind of writer you are. People will ask you. They aren't testing you. They really want to know because what you write might be able to help them somehow.

Identify yourself as a writer. Don't worry about what other people think or say.

What do I do if they laugh?

Some people poked fun when I said I was a writer. I'll admit that it shook my confidence. They asked if I was a millionaire or if I had been on TV or if I'd spoken to Oprah recently. You'll get lots of responses. But most people just wanted to know what I wrote. Be ready with an answer. Because I still didn't take myself seriously, my answer was vague for a long time. If you aren't taking yourself seriously, nobody else will either.

Believe. You are a writer because you are. A writer is someone who writes. Better yet, a writer is someone who writes and publishes. The key words here are "published writer." Should I still call myself a writer even if I'm working on my first book? That is entirely up to you. But why not? If anything, it'll add accountability to your mission and get you working harder and faster to deliver your material.

I once lacked confidence and clarity in what I was doing and who I really was. When I connected with my identity, there was no question. I wanted to be a full-time writer and an online educator. And I knew that I could no longer hide this from anyone if I wanted to live this dream. Like a genie in a bottle, I unleashed my magic and set myself free.

Now it's your turn. **Set yourself free** and write the story inside you that is struggling to break out.

The Struggle with Transparency

"Every secret of a writer's soul, every experience of his life, every quality of his mind, is written large in his works."

— Virginia Woolf

Many writers avoid being transparent when they experience rejection, much like anyone else. Instead of putting ourselves out there and pushing our brand, we tend to hide from the world. Transparency creates feelings of vulnerability, and because writers tend to be introverts, vulnerability is what we want to avoid.

But avoiding people is the same as writing and then not publishing. The moment our content is visible, transparency is what we're all about, not invisibility.

For example, you avoid doing interviews or podcasts because you might say something stupid or look foolish. This isn't to say we have to give up being introverts. It's not a bad thing. But there are many times that stepping out of that shell, even for just a brief moment, can have a powerful impact on our careers as authors.

When I write, I go into introversion mode. I can shut off and nobody will bother me during this time. But when it is time to share a message, you should give it all you have. It means striking a fine balance between isolating to write, and then stepping out into the world.

As an author building your image, your story is everything. Although readers may take an interest in your books and what you have to say or teach, what they really want to know more about is you.

Yes, you.

As one author told me once, "If you want to build a following of loyal fans, you have to show them who you are. You won't get far if you hide behind a veil of words. They want more from authors these days. With social media and technology, everyone is on stage. This is a great opportunity for you to connect with people."

Consider telling your fans your story. What is it about you that stands apart from others? What makes you unique? The answer is everything. There is only one of you. Maybe. How are you going to tell your story in a way that intrigues people?

Six Ways to Stand Out and Tell Your Story

1. Resist the urge to sound like a textbook or salesperson.

When communicating with your readers through an email or blog post, leave out your ego. You can't just send out sales copy. People won't buy it and your message won't be read.

Instead, relax and be yourself. Let your ideas flow freely. This will create a deeper level of transparency. You'll get more subscribers because your current list will recommend and share your message with their tribe.

Resist 'talking down' to your readers or trying to be too clever. At the end of the day, most people want an experience they can connect with and a message they can take to heart and draw a lesson from.

2. Talk about one major struggle you had to overcome.

People love stories. Most of all, they want stories that are inspiring and told from the point of view of someone who has lived what they are going through. People who are struggling want to walk with you on the journey.

By sharing your struggles, you are giving readers and fans something they're all looking for: hope. You can do this whether you write fiction or nonfiction. Tell your audience why you can deliver the content they want. What makes your story special? What makes you unique?

Then, once you figure that out...

3. Tell your readers how you can help them succeed.

Your readers are signing up for your blog, website, or buying your books for a reason. If you don't know that reason, you don't know your readers. How do you know what they want? Ask.

Send out a group email to your list, even if there are only ten people on it. As Jeff Goins said, "If there are ten people on your list, that's your list. Focus on delivering value-driven content and focus on what will help your readers succeed." After all, isn't that what we want? To push our potential up and beyond what it is now? Your mission as an author is to take your readers on a journey.

Mark Dawson does this with his fiction series. Gary Keller does this with his bestselling book, *The One Thing*. I could name hundreds of authors who have built their platforms by giving readers what they want.

When you provide value and make that your primary focus, both you and your readers will succeed. As Zig Ziglar said, "If you help enough people get what they want, you will also get what you want."

4. Learn from keynote speakers and authority figures who have been there. A big part of your purpose as an author is to always be improving yourself. This is what international business guru Tony Robbins calls *CANI: Constant and Never-Ending Improvement.*

For example, spending thirty minutes a day improving yourself and focusing on the areas you need to strengthen is one way to do this. When you concentrate on making yourself better, you are committed to helping your audience become better, too. After all, how can they learn from you if you are not showing that you, too, can change?

Again, this is self-evident through writing books, blogging, or releasing regular video content. With today's technology, we are without boundaries or limits—but we are held back by our own limitations. I always learn by following those who are at a level I aspire to reach.

If you are a fiction writer, you probably have your own short list of writers you follow: Stephen King, J.K. Rowling, James Patterson, Nora Roberts, or Agatha Christie.

If you write nonfiction, depending on the category, you could be looking up to writers like Brandon Burchard, Tim Ferris, or Malcolm Gladwell.

Learn from the masters of the craft who are out there creating, promoting, and teaching what they know. One suggestion is to choose a favorite author and model the way they write. How do they communicate with readers?

By modeling the author you admire, you can gain a stronger understanding of how they present their work. Of course, you want to create your own style eventually, but to get started you can use a writer as your working role model.

5. Be honest. You are probably an honest person, so you are thinking, "What does he mean by that?" I recently read an email from a big influencer in which he described some difficult times. This is someone with a list of 50,000-plus subscribers. When he posted his problems on his website, do you think a ton of people thought he was weak and unsubscribed? No. He had hundreds of comments on his post that included prayers, wishes, and words of encouragement from readers.

People genuinely want to help each other, but sometimes they're afraid to. They don't want to admit they are in pain or need help. What if it backfires? What if I come across sounding like I'm whining? Well, if you are indeed complaining and stirring up a controversial topic, you'll get that reaction.

But remember that being honest with your community makes them feel as if they're part of a solid team.

A good example of this is Hal Elrod and his *Miracle Morning Community*. Hal Elrod, bestselling author and keynote speaker, was diagnosed with cancer in December of 2016. Instead of hiding and downplaying it, Hal opened up to his community and shared details of the battle he was about to undertake. The community has become a strong league of positive and inspirational people bonding together to help each other (and Hal) overcome their struggles.

When you share your transparency with your audience, they will love you for it. Successful authors, entrepreneurs, podcasters, and bloggers connect with their audience by holding nothing back. How do you do this?

6. Tell your story. Share your vision of the world you are striving to create for yourself, your family, and your audience. Give them a big taste of what they'll get by sticking with you on the journey. Not only will this instill greater confidence in your following, but it will gradually remove any uncertainty you have in yourself as an author.

Those who have anxiety about their craft are struggling with the truth. They stress about saying the right thing, being the right person, or making a mistake and trying to target everyone as their audience. But your audience will gravitate toward your message. They'll read your blogs, buy your books, and purchase your courses.

This will happen only if you can be the transparent leader people want you to be. This is a big challenge. Right away we think we'll be rejected if we just be ourselves. We have fear of vulnerability. What if someone calls you out and dismisses your opinion? How will you deal with it? What if you get a hostile comment on social media or a negative review of your book?

In many situations we shrink away from appearing vulnerable. It can be a terrifying experience. What if I appear less confident? What if they see me as the fraud I am?

We hold back from transparency for the same reasons we avoid the possibility of brining on rejection: If others see us for who we really are, they may not accept us. But is the problem with other people, or is it with us?

Willing to be Vulnerable

The willingness to be vulnerability is a positive decision. It is our vulnerability that readers crave. After all, emotional vulnerability connects you to yourself, and when that happens, it connects you to your writing on a new level.

By admitting you are vulnerable as a writer and being okay with that, you are not trying to hold yourself back. Readers can pick up on a writer when he or she is restraining from telling more.

You are a teacher and story teller. If you write fiction, you have to be vulnerable for your characters. If you write nonfiction, you should be vulnerable, so readers can connect with you on the same level. Be the type of writer that your audience expects. Avoid the temptation to rise above and be the voice of all reason and knowing. You can still be an authority without trying to fake that you know everything. Making the decision to be vulnerable with your readers is the first step to forming a long-lasting relationship.

After all, realize that we are not in the people-pleasing game. If you try to please everyone, you end up helping nobody. You walk on eggshells, careful not break any. But the boat that gets rocked causes ripples.

Part of building your image and giving yourself permission to be a writer is the freedom to voice your opinion, to teach, to share your values and principles with your tribe.

Transparency isn't about opening yourself up to vulnerability or the chance of being injured; it is the opportunity to connect with people on an emotional level. It is about building trust. Once trust is there, the relationship with your audience has a foundation to build upon.

Building Transparency: An Exercise

Brainstorm strategies you can implement to be more transparent with your brand. How can you share your writing on a new level that reaches more people? We live in a modern world of communication where anything is possible, and we could reach thousands of people in an instant.

For example:

- Start an Instagram account and post pictures of your day as an author, and create reels recording your insights while sharing depths of wisdom

- Get into the habit of shooting video and start up a YouTube channel.

- Post your videos to your website or on Vimeo.

- Blog about your current writing project.

- When you launch your next book, give early readers an inside look at how you wrote it.

Make a list of the things that you're afraid to share with people. What are you holding back? If you were to open up about this, would it connect you with your readers on a wider platform? I am not suggesting you open up about everything, but you have to decide the level of transparency you are comfortable with.

Embracing Uncertainty and Facing Your Writing Fears

"A blank piece of paper is God's way of telling us how hard it is to be God."

— Sidney Sheldon

You are a **writer**.

Just think about those words for a moment. Repeat this to yourself several times.

I am a writer.

But are you really? Do you actually believe this? Are you still working on your first book and have yet to publish anything?

I know what this is like. It's hard to take yourself seriously when you haven't made a dime on writing and people are looking at you saying, "Well, when is the money rolling in?"

Your greatest fear is the moment before the writing is on the page. You might experience fear while an idea is lodged in your head, just swimming around, looking for permission to be set free.

As a writer, it is your mission to put all those ideas, good and bad, down on paper. Get them out there. Let the world judge, critique, and form an opinion. It is better than staying silent and suffering with the reality of never putting yourself out there.

So, what is a writer? How would you define someone who calls themselves an author? How many books does it take before you feel comfortable saying you are a writer? How much money would you have to be making? What status would you need to achieve?

Many aspiring authors feel a sense of shame when they identify themselves as an author. Why? People look at you differently, as if you have some special talent or gift. The only talent that I know of is called hard work.

So, why do we have doubts, fears, and uncertainties about ourselves as authors?

When it comes to writing a book, it is hard to admit that you're a writer if you are just starting out, have never published, and the writing habit hasn't taken hold yet.

I had already written several books before I could admit this to myself. It was really tough. I wasn't a New York Times bestselling author. I had sold barely a hundred books even after several years. I made a lot of mistakes and didn't take action toward the areas of the business I should have.

But I was writing. Still, there's another part to becoming a writer. Writers eventually have completed works. When you tell people that you are a writer, the first thing they'll ask you is:

"What kind of books do you write?"

The second question they'll ask is: "Where can I find these books?"

Again, whether it's a blog or a book, there are many writers who publish content for which they get paid.

The Writing Hobby

For many years, writing was just my hobby. This was how I identified the profession if anyone asked. After all, I wasn't making much money on it, and until you publish something people are going to buy, you won't make any money from your writing. Writing for publication has three phases.

Write.

Publish.

Repeat.

As writers, we deal with several conflicting emotions, most of them in the form of beliefs we have internalized as hard-boiled truths. Writers are famous people who have to starve and exhaust themselves before they can qualify as an author.

But in today's world, that just isn't true.

It can be done. It is being done every day. But if you are a writer, I assume that writing isn't something you have to do. It's a driving force in your life that cannot be stopped. Most professional writers are professionals because they practice their craft every day.

One of the best habits you could develop right now is the writing habit. If you want to break your fears, get through the procrastination, and climb over the hurdles of getting your books out there, commit to writing every day. Later in this book, I'll get into this habit in more depth.

But even if you are writing every day, there lurks in the background a question that makes or breaks most writers. It is just a whisper at times, but it's there in everything we do.

That question is: "Am I good enough?"

Good enough to write? Good enough to call myself a writer?

It creates doubt, uncertainty and ultimately builds into our fears that we are not good enough for the quest of our dreams. If you are an aspiring author who hasn't published anything yet, this is an obstacle you will likely come up against again and again.

If you are a published author, while you may have a routine that works for you, writing a new book is challenging because we want to do better on the next one than the last. We want to take our craft to a new level, to make our writing better.

And if you're a published author who has multiple bestsellers, you will still come up against this. Even after publishing my fourth book, I doubted my talent and ability to be any good at what I did.

I asked a mentor of mine, "How will I reach that point of feeling good enough?"

"You're already there," he said. "You just haven't given yourself permission to be that good at what you do."

So, give yourself permission to be a writer.

What we search for is validation. We want someone to show up and give us a badge that says, "successful author" and then maybe we'll have earned the right to be good enough.

But self-doubt is part of the journey. It's there with each new writing project, waiting to be invited in and cause a disruptive wave in your writing career. The key to dealing with this is to work through the doubt and uncertainty. Push through it.

There are no magic pills or easy trails. The best way to push through doubt is to push those words onto the paper. Even if they are terrible. Especially if it's bad writing. You can edit bad writing, but there isn't much you can do with a blank page.

Most words in a first draft are random thoughts without much structure. So, give yourself permission to write badly. Allow the creative process to come through, no matter how absurd it may seem.

Fear is here to stay. It will always be with you, not just as a writer, but in most challenges you take in life. Try doing something that's new to you. Can you avoid feeling fear because you might fail? No. It's natural.

Fear and self-doubt are always present, but the power they have over you is in correlation to the amount of action you take.

Attitude will be a deciding factor. If you let the doubt win, you'll be shelving your ideas before you even begin. Your voice needs to be heard. You have a message, a story, and a sense of purpose to share with people. If you fail to deliver, your fear of failure will cripple your spirit. I'd rather work through the fear and see what is on the other side.

Wouldn't you?

Our uncertainty stems from the belief that the work we produce will suck and that nobody will want to read what we have written.

Don't let this stop you from creating. If you are driven to write a book, or multiple books, it begins with accepting the fear for what it is: a driving force that can be turned into your greatest ally. Authors are often overwhelmed and defeated when the fear becomes bigger than the dream.

The fear isn't the obstacle. The fear is the fuel that pushes you through the tough spots. When you feel doubt creep in, that is a good thing. It is a sign that you are challenging yourself to a goal that means something. The reason you're afraid of failing is because it matters to you.

*"**A** book is made from a tree. It is an assemblage of flat, flexible parts (still called "leaves") imprinted with dark pigmented squiggles. One glance at it and you hear the voice of another person, perhaps someone dead for thousands of years. Across the millennia, the author is speaking, clearly and silently, inside your head, directly to you. Writing is perhaps the greatest of human inventions, binding together people, and citizens of distant epochs, who never knew one another. Books break the shackles of time--proof that humans can work magic."*

— **Carl Sagan**

Creating Your Writing Space

"The writer is an explorer.
Every step is an advance into a new land."

— Ralph Waldo Emerson

Identifying yourself as an author is a critical part of the process because it builds confidence and keeps the fear of rejection on the outside where it belongs. But one of the best ways you can build greater confidence is to create a motivating, dynamic writing environment.

When I started to get serious about writing, I realized I needed to set up a more professional studio for writing. My current situation was cluttered, disorganized, and not very comfortable. I set up a writing room with all the right prompts. I turned my living space into a writer's laboratory.

Your writing environment plays a critical role in your life as an author. If you write in a place that's full of noise, uncomfortable to be in, or affects your emotional state to the point you don't want to do anything, you might consider your environment needs some work.

Over the years, I have learned to recognize what works and what doesn't when it comes to preparing myself for pounding out those words.

Here is a list of factors that, if handled the right way, can boost your productivity as a writer and encourage you to stay in the zone.

Display Your Favorite Author Photos

I printed out photographs of my favorite authors and posted them around my desk and on one wall. I used the pictures of famous authors such as Stephen King, Tom Clancy, and J.K. Rowling. These photos had a strong impact on my mood. If my confidence waned or I needed to think about what I was writing, I'd have a conversation with one of the authors sharing my space. It helps to get the ideas churning again and puts you back in the game.

Find at least twenty photos of authors you want to emulate. Print these out if you can and place them around your room. An alternative idea is to use the photos as screensavers or a desktop screen. You can change the photo every day if you like. There is nothing like writing and having your favorite author looking back at you as if to say, "Come on, you've got this!"

Post Author Quotes

You can feel very inspired by setting up your workspace with author quotes, as well. This book you are reading is full of quotes by well-known authors to inspire you.

Hang Up a Yearly Calendar

Your book will get written faster if you have goals for each day and week. The best way to manage this is by scheduling your time on a calendar. Schedule every hour that you commit to your author business. *What gets scheduled, gets done.*

As Bob Goff said, "The battle for happiness begins on the pages of our calendars."

Buy a big wall calendar. Have enough space on each day that you can write down your goals for that day. When you have a goal for that day or week, write it down or use a sticky note. Sticky notes work well because you can move them around if you need to change the dates on your goals.

The calendar is a simple yet highly effective method for staying on track and maintaining your writing productivity. If you schedule your work and remain disciplined, the work will get done.

Music for Mood

Many authors can write to the sound of their favorite tunes. Is there anything that gets you working faster? Do you write better with deeper focus when listening to rock music or classical? I set up several playlists that I use depending on the kind of writing I am doing.

If I need to concentrate deeply, I'll go with something more soothing or soft. When I write furiously, and the pace is fast, I can speed up the tone of the music.

Writing Surface and Chair

There are two types of desks and you should consider setting up your writing area with access to both.

The standing desk. This is fast becoming popular for many reasons. Sitting down for long periods of time becomes uncomfortable and unhealthy. You can balance your online time between sitting and standing. For example, when I have a three-hour writing session, I do 50/50.

For sitting, you want a chair that is comfortable but not too comfortable. I personally prefer a simple non-swivel stool when sitting down to write. It is designed so that you have to sit up straight. If there is a comfortable back attached, as with most chairs, you tend to get sleepy. This can trigger other habits as well, such as craving television.

Creating a Clutter-Free Environment

If there is any one factor that will slow you down or kill your motivation, it is a room full of clutter. I used to work in a very cramped room with out-of-date papers lying around, Post-It notes scattered haphazardly, and decorations that took up space.

If your room looks like this, it can have a serious impact on your emotional state. I believe that what you see around you occupies a space in your mind. Unfinished business is unconsciously recorded in your mind and this leads to clutter both physical and mental.

Although we can't always be in complete control of our physical space, especially if we're living with other people, you can get rid of any clutter you have control over. Go for a simple workplace that makes you feel relaxed.

Take one day to clean out your room. Get rid of anything that isn't conducive to your lifestyle as a writer. Either keep it, sell it, or get rid of it.

Creating Your Distraction-Free Zone

Within a few weeks I had a room that looked like a writer lived there. This was especially useful during those times in the writing process when I needed a distraction-free zone.

You may be asking, "Okay, what does any of this have to do with feeling rejected?" Well, over the years I discovered that part of the reason I struggled was because I didn't identify myself as an author.

As I mentioned earlier, creating that author identity is critical to stimulating action. By surrounding yourself with the "write stuff," you'll be able to connect with the writer within. It is this connection you create that will fill you with energy and enthusiasm for mastering your writing.

Your Digital Environment

Just as your physical environment plays a big role in your life as an author, a cluttered desktop is going to lead to massive distraction when you try to stay focused on getting things done.

Do a complete dump of all the files slowing down your computer's performance. Back up files in **iCloud** or **Dropbox**. Keep your desktop relatively clutter-free. You won't waste time searching for material or constantly moving files around.

Here are the steps again for creating a **dynamic writing environment**:

1. Remove all the unnecessary clutter from your environment.

2. Set up a music playlist for your writing sessions, if it inspires you.

3. Set up your equipment for comfort. Get comfortable, but not too relaxed.

4. Keep your writing environment distraction-free.

5. Pin up author photos and positive quotes. Decorate your area with photos of authors you love and quotes that inspire you.

6. Buy a large calendar and use it to schedule your goals with Post-It notes.

Stick to a Writing Routine

"When I'm in writing mode for a novel, I get up at four a.m. and work for five to six hours. In the afternoon, I run for ten kilometers or swim for fifteen hundred meters (or do both), then I read a bit and listen to some music. I go to bed at nine p.m."

— Haruki Murakami

Authors often use a set formula that helps them write. Having a daily word count and creating the writing habit is essential to building your writing platform. Today, you can set up a writing routine that works for you.

A routine is set of habits that we follow to achieve a specific outcome. It is the same as any other routine. When I go to the gym, I follow a routine for working on cardio, and then I have another routine for building muscle mass. If the routine gets old, I can tweak it to meet the demands of my environment.

Your writing routine will have a large role to play when it comes to finishing your book.

Well, now you can add writing to the list of daily habits. To do this, we'll need to force feed it for about twenty-eight days. According to Charles Duhigg, author of the best-selling book *The Power of Habit*, it takes about sixty days for a habit to become a daily routine.

Exercise before and during your writing. Listen to music while writing. Write in your favorite location, away from the hustle of everyday life. Your routine may include these habits.

Write in your favorite place

Establish the place you feel most comfortable writing. This doesn't mean it has to be someplace quiet. You might write in the living room surrounded by family disruption and noise like E.B. White, author of *Charlotte's Web*.

E.B. White said:

My house has a living room that is at the core of everything that goes on: it is a passageway to the cellar, to the kitchen, to the closet where the phone lives. There's a lot of traffic. But it's a bright, cheerful room, and I often use it as a room to write in, despite the carnival that is going on all around me.

Seek out the place where you can be most productive and feel most confident, somewhere that's totally comfortable for you. This could be a solitary room or a busy café. You might divide your writing time between several places. Wherever you set up, make sure you have access to all the tools you need.

Leo Tolstoy, the famed Russian author of *War and Peace*, locked himself in isolation and nobody was allowed to disturb him during this time. Will you write in a busy environment, or will you lock yourself away and avoid contact with anyone else while writing?

Where will you set up your writing spot?

What does this place look like?

Can you focus in this location?

Stick to a consistent schedule

Stephen King sits down to write every morning from eight to eight-thirty. It was his way of programming his brain to get ready for the day's work. He writes an average of ten pages a day.

Haruki Murakami wakes up at four a.m. and works for five to six hours.

W.H. Auden would rise at six a.m. and would work hard from seven to eleven-thirty, when his mind was sharpest.

What time are you committed to writing every day? At what hour is your mind the sharpest? When do you feel the most productive? If you can, writing at the same time daily sets the tone for your writing productivity. Will you write six pages a day (2,000 words) like Stephen King, or 10,000 words a day like Michael Crichton?

Commit to a time of day and a length of time during which to write. Set a goal for yourself and try to hit the target every day by sticking with your routine.

What time will you write tomorrow?

How much will you write?

What do you have to do to set yourself up with this routine?

Meditate, exercise, or do yoga to relax before writing. Get into a state of readiness for writing.

Many authors talk about reaching a deeper state of mind and relaxation as they get into their writing. It can be difficult to simply show up at your desk every day. You might be feeling anxious. Maybe something is on your mind, or you're fidgety for some reason.

If your mindset is off, you may not feel the creative presence needed to get started. Many writers struggle to start writing because they haven't prepared themselves mentally for the writing session. Part of your routine should be focused on preparing your mind and body for the writing session.

Focus on one project until it's finished

Henry Miller, the famed author of *The Tropic of Capricorn*, once created a work schedule that included the steps to his daily routine. The first step, as listed in his book *Henry Miller on Writing*, is: *Work on one thing at a time until finished.*

Trying to multi-task or juggle projects while working on one book is going to slow things down. It is challenging to stay focused on one project, especially if you have ideas for multiple books or perhaps you are blogging along with writing a book.

This isn't to say that you should work on only one book at a time, but when you commit an hour or two hours to writing, stick with one project during that time. Realistically we all have multiple projects to work on. To manage this, block in your time for working on one book. Hit your goal for that day and move on to the next thing.

This leads us to the next strategy.

Set up a timer when you write

Whatever routine you decide to follow, remember that the focus is on preparing to write. Some people can wake up early and be very productive in the morning. Others like to stay up late and do their best work in the twilight hours. The routine you implement will be your method to building a successful career as an author.

Or, as J.K. Rowling said, "Sometimes you have to get your writing done in spare moments here and there. I can write anywhere. I made up the names of the characters on a sick bag while I was on an airplane."

Create a routine that works for you. Wake up early, stay up late, eat well, or drink a glass of fruit juice before you write. Take frequent breaks if your writing stints are long.

So, this brings us to a few questions: What is your ideal writing routine? How do you visualize yourself performing at your best? Will you combine exercise with long periods of writing? Will you practice visual imagery for ten minutes before getting started?

For great ideas on building structure into your day, you can read this blog post by **Atomic Habits** bestselling author James Clear: The Daily Routines of 12 Famous Writers.

Building a Foundation for Bulletproof Confidence

"Writing a book is a horrible, exhausting struggle, like a long bout of some painful illness. One would never undertake such a thing if one were not driven on by some demon whom one can neither resist nor understand."

— George Orwell

You don't have to be brave to write a book. You just need some basic organization, a good idea, and something you can write about for 20 to 30,000 words. If you are like most writers, you'll begin with less confidence than you had intended. That's okay. Confidence is what comes with practice, and the more you work at it, the better you'll get. Soon you'll show up every day to write without really thinking about it.

I know this sounds like motivational fluff, but there's one thing I have seen again and again while working with authors: Those who finished their books worked almost every day no matter how little confidence they felt. On my worst days, I took extra time to read some inspirational quotes or literature and spent more time than usual warming up with practice writing.

Here are four strategies to prime up your confidence for writing on those days when you don't feel like writing anything at all.

Confidence Builder #1: Stick with What You Know and Avoid Lengthy Research

It is easy to get bogged down in the details of research. When I am starting a new book, the first thing I want to do is read all the books out there related to the topic I am writing about.

There are two problems with this. First of all, you could get lost in weeks or even months of endless research before you write anything. This is only damaging your confidence as an author because you won't actually get any writing done.

If you have to, do some light research in the beginning—just enough to get started—but don't cram your head with hundreds of pages of text right away.

All you need to start writing is a basic idea of what your chapter is about. Then, write about that thought. Write about what you know first. Think of it as telling a story to someone. Maybe they asked whether you knew anything about this subject. Imagine telling them about your idea, your thoughts, and your opinion on the topic.

Writing about it isn't any different, but as soon as we label ourselves as writers, it shifts the mindset from casual conversationalist to serious writer who has to get the facts straight. In the polished version of your book, yes, you want the facts to be right. But in this first draft, focus on the words only. Research the numbers later.

During conversations with your friends or family, when they ask you a question you aren't totally sure about, how often do you say, "Just a second, let me go research that and get back to you in a day or two." If you're like me, you give the answer you think is right, and then you can check on the actual facts later.

When it comes to writing, it's easy to get tied down in checking facts, typing questions into Google, reading blog posts, or buying niche-related books on Kindle. I know, I've done all of this, and the one thing that always got in the way of actually writing anything was thinking I had to be an authority on the subject before I could write about it.

But actually, the opposite is true.

Whatever topic I am writing about, whether it's how to live an empowered lifestyle or overcoming rejection (two things I know a lot about) I discovered how to talk about it during the writing process. I researched these topics, but no matter how much I read, it didn't make me feel any more confidence. Just more anxious. How could I sound like Tony Robbins or Brian Tracy? My writing will never be as good as Hemingway's. Researching is a necessary element for writing, but it can also be an endless rabbit hole.

Lesson #1: Being the authority means writing about something you are passionate about and knowing a lot more at the end of the book than when you started. In other words, you become the authority as you write. Not before.

1. Write what you know first. This will always be polished later.

2. Set a date for when the writing starts. Is it tomorrow? The day after? In five minutes? I set a time for each day. Sometimes this planned event gets interrupted and I have to work around my family schedule, but that is the great thing about setting your own work schedule. You can move it around.

3. Decide the material you will read for your research. Narrow it down to just a couple books, a few blog posts, or a set number of interviews. You don't have to read everything. Remember that authority comes with writing the book, not before writing it.

Confidence Builder #2: Write in Your Own Voice

When I wrote my first personal development book, it took nearly three years to complete. And even after finishing it, I wasn't really happy with it. The book was a hard feat, weighing in at nearly 90,000 words. That is a lot for a book that I had no idea what I was going to do with. But I didn't necessarily struggle because of the writing. It was my lack of clarity when it came to my own voice as a writer.

As it turns out, I didn't have one.

The material I had written came across as a cheap rip-off from the books I'd read in my research. It just wasn't original. The writing was mine, and the ideas were mine, but it sounded too much like a textbook, as if I'd been making an attempt to sound cleverer than I was.

It occurred to me that one of the reasons writing is so hard is because we show up to write thinking we have to create perfect prose and the best sentences, like Ernest Hemingway, Stephen King, or Agatha Christie. I mean, they've sold millions of books. So, if I write like my favorite authors, it shouldn't be a problem.

Lack of originality is always transparent. If you have ever delivered a speech, you'll know the best speeches are when the speaker delivers from the cuff. They are original and not fixed on a script in front of them.

Well, the same can work for writing. We gain greater confidence in our writing skills when we can just show up and be ourselves. Trying to be a perfect writer is going to crush your confidence as soon as you start to second-guess your talent.

Discovering your voice is a powerful confidence builder. The day I found my voice, I no longer had a fear of writing. I decided to just show up and tell the story. I had a light script (the outline) but the rest was all me.

To bring this voice out, I visualized myself on stage, speaking in front of a group of friends and sharing my message. As I visualized myself doing this, my fingers were working across the keyboard, writing down what I said. You can try this, but you might discover your own way to bring out your unique voice.

Another strategy involves recording your thoughts with an app. Speak first, and then either transcribe or write it down later. You should focus on developing your voice as you write. Once you tap into this side of yourself, the words will flow much faster.

Lesson #2: Writing in your own voice means telling the story from your own point of view. Two people can tell the same joke and receive completely different reactions from the crowd. Be original. Be authentic.

1. Write in your own voice. Be wary of mimicking other authors you admire.

2. Develop this voice by speaking your thoughts out loud.

3. Visualize delivering your message on stage to an audience of people who paid good money to hear you speak.

4. Take a video of yourself or use Facebook Live and get accustomed to talking to your crowd.

Robert Benchley said, "It took me fifteen years to discover I had no talent for writing, but I couldn't give it up because by that time I was too famous."

Confidence Builder #3: Set Up Short, Actionable Goals

Today, your goal is to write 5,000 words. Ready?

Maybe not. That is a lot of writing. Some people claim they can do that in one hour. For others, that is a week's worth of writing. But starting off with a high-end goal is not a confidence booster.

First of all, you might fail to reach your target goal. Anything can happen. You might run into a block. Maybe the kids have a big soccer tournament coming up, or perhaps you're just worn out from day-to-day lifestyle activities. Then, when you don't achieve that goal of 5,000 words, you might beat yourself up for it.

Small, actionable, achievable goals build your confidence as a writer. Can you write 500 words in an hour? How about 1,000?

I generally target 1,000 words a day. It isn't an overly ambitious goal, but I know I can hit it with just one hour of focused writing a day. I am a slow typist, averaging thirty words a minute. I type with two fingers because I can't type well. Yes, you read that right. I have written eleven books and I can't type properly. But by creating short time blocks of thirty minutes, I can get around 400 words written.

Lesson #3: Set up short, writing focused time-blocks. This strategy works very well. Set up a timer for as long as you want. I recommend twenty-five or thirty minutes. You can use the Pomodoro Technique, in which you work on one focused task for twenty-five minutes, take a five-minute break, and then dive in for another twenty-five minutes. It works, and you can stay focused for just twenty-five minutes.

You can write at any pace that makes you comfortable. Set a goal of five hundred words per day to start. This mini-goal is easily attainable. Try two mini sessions and write 250 words each time.

When you consider your book could be 20—25,000 words at a minimum, the writing process feels like a daunting mountain to climb. It may seem like the peak of Everest and you might wonder, "How am I going to scale that?" The trick is to take your mind off the peak. Focus on the next plateau, which is only a few meters above you. That much you can manage.

Lesson #4: Large goals are disempowering when they appear unattainable. You can achieve anything if you break it down into manageable chunks with short, productive sessions.

1. Track your word count in an Excel sheet. If you write five hundred words a day, while that doesn't sound like a lot, after sixty days it's the first draft of your book. On some days, you'll do more, and you'll be done in even less time.

2. Set up your writing sessions in short bursts. How long does it take you to write two hundred words? Use the Pomodoro technique discussed earlier. In three sessions, using this technique, I can easily reach one thousand words in one day. So can you.

3. Once you start hitting your goals, increase the goal by small margins. Take it from five hundred words a day to 750. If that starts to get easy, increase it to one thousand. Just like a muscle, you can make it grow with consistent "workouts."

Confidence Builder #4: The Half-Finished Book

Do you know what a half-finished book has in common with a book that hasn't been started yet? Neither of them can be published. Only finished books can be published. I'll admit that I've started many projects and never carried them through. Or, I let the project drag out for months or even years before deciding it had to be finished. But half-built bridges are useless. If we can't cross to the other side, what is the point?

When it comes to your writing, finishing what you started is an immense confidence builder. But I am not just talking about completing the entire book itself. Let's break this down into manageable chunks. How about completing just a chapter? It wasn't just finishing a book that made me a confident author. It was the completion of each chapter that helped me built more motivation to keep going.

We have to complete our sentences before we complete the paragraph—paragraphs before pages, and pages before chapters. Each of these is a mini-achievement that can build your confidence as you move through your work.

Focus on one writing task at a time. This might sound like common sense. After all, who in their right mind would try writing two or even three books at the same time? Well, I did. I had so many projects going at once that every day it was like changing my clothes four times.

How many did I finish? None of them. How did I feel? Worn-out and frustrated. Why? I wasn't going to finish three books in a month. So, I put aside the two projects that would have to wait and focused on the one that mattered. I finished. My confidence increased. Lesson learned.

Finish what you start. If you set out to write a chapter, finish that chapter. If you get stuck and you have to come back to it later, that's fine, but finish within a certain time period. Don't let it hang around. Your bundle of unfinished projects will be on your mind even when you're sleeping.

Lesson #5: Finish what you started. If you couldn't finish it today, put it on your list for tomorrow. Get it done and move on.

1. Make a list of projects you haven't finished. Then, focus on each of them one by one and get to work. Stay focused on a single project until it is finished.

2. Get into the habit of calling yourself a finisher.

Strategies for Beating Procrastination

"I went for years not finishing anything. Because, of course, when you finish something you can be judged."

— Erica Jong

The first challenge in writing a book is starting. This can cause stress, nervousness, and instill fear of failure. As if committing our thoughts to the screen makes them real. And yet, if you had to talk about the same topic to someone, you could probably do it very easily. Right?

One strategy that works well for me is to start each writing session with ten minutes of "speaking my book" and using software such as **Dragonspeak** or **Speakit**. The most difficult part of the writing process is getting started. We're often met with a heavy resistance that shows up at the beginning of each writing session.

If we procrastinate, we walk away for the moment and most likely won't return. Before you decide to take a break from having done nothing, there are a few simple tricks (if I dare call them that because they are so easy) you can employ to get that mini-snowball moving.

Resistance to writing is one of the hurdles that slow down most writers. It isn't because writing is hard, but rather, several variables come into play when we get down to creating. Do you struggle with trying to write the perfect prose? Do you feel unprepared? Is there a voice of self-doubt that holds you back? Are you already thinking your book will be terrible?

A host of negative thoughts can cause procrastination. That's why, in order to get through the initial stage of self-rejection and the resulting resistance that shows up, I have put together a small checklist to help you get started.

Each day, and before every writing session, you can get ready and warmed up with this checklist. The purpose is to get you into the flow of writing in order to combat negative feelings that cause resistance to your creative ambition.

Self-Rejection: After the Book Launch

You have worked for months on your book, finished editing it yourself, and then you sent it to your editor. Breaking past all fears, you published your book after all the pain and sweat of working on your masterpiece. It is now out there. People are reading it and the excitement of the launch is fading.

This is when many new authors face the reality of the self-publishing world. Not to crush your big moment, but now you might be thinking: Will I continue to write books? Do I want to write another book? Can I make a living as a writer? How many books do I have to write before I can make it?

This is the stage when self-rejection starts to appear. Your book rankings might have fallen, and you've watched everything you worked for tumble down to a few dollars in royalties.

The first thing we do is blame ourselves.

My book must be pretty bad.

Not that many people liked it.

I got two bad reviews.

If only I could do this again.

There are a lot of conflicting emotions. We feel rejected and burned. We want to keep pushing forward but....

At some point, you're going to go through the highs and lows of writing your book. There will be those days when you feel unbreakable and the ideas are coming faster than you can get them down on paper. You have just written ten thousand words and you only have fifteen thousand more to go. Nothing can stop you now.

Then you hit a wall. You don't feel like writing. You get stuck on a chapter. Or maybe you made the fatal error of going back and re-reading some of your earlier work and you've drawn the conclusion that it sucks. It's a first draft, after all. You had momentum last week and this week you can barely look at a keyboard.

Some people mistake this for writer's block, but what you've really come up against is self-doubt. It happens to everyone. There will come a point when we lose our confidence and the book we are certain is a grand masterpiece will seem no better than a sixth-grader's essay.

Losing momentum is part of the process. It will happen even when you start out strong. But this doesn't mean you have to give in. Momentum can be likened to motivation. When we rely on motivation or willpower, we are allowing our emotions to navigate for us. But what about when you're working in a real job that pays the bills?

You probably lose momentum and motivation several times during a work day. Do you drop everything and go home? Do you give up? Chances are if you did you'd be unemployed. So why is it that when we're writing a book, losing momentum or motivation sets us back? We might put it off or even shelve the manuscript.

Six tips to stay focused and keep building momentum

1. Review your outline. Return to your outline (you have one, right?) and read through the topics of each chapter. Get a feel for the book's content again and let the ideas slowly work their way into your mind. Then focus on the chapter you're working on.

If you haven't chosen that chapter, do it now. Lack of concentration is one reason writers stumble. They show up without knowing what they'll write about for the day. Your outline is the roadmap for your book. Make it as detailed as you can, and you'll get finished faster.

2. Abstain from mindless net searching and make time.

Do you ever find yourself scanning and scrolling just for the hell of it? Jumping from site to site looking for something interesting? It's a habit that feeds into procrastination. It kills precious time that you don't have.

Don't start checking email or surfing Amazon for book deals every time you sit down to write. **You are here to write**. If it helps, make this writing time the same every day. If you keep moving the goal post, you won't score as much. In other words, a habit that is intentional is the best kind of practice.

You are not supposed to find the time for writing—you should make the time. You can wake up one-hour early and write from five to six before you start the day. You can write at night after the family is in bed. But whenever you do it, make a serious effort to do it at the same time every day. If you can't do it at the same time, make a serious effort to grab pockets of time when you can.

If there's a day that you can't write at the same time, schedule it for another time. There will be days like this, but you can still commit to the writing hour.

If you are in the habit of checking email or diving into the net for entertainment as soon as you sit down, set up a positive trigger when you stop yourself from acting out. Pay yourself one dollar every time you decide not to give in to your weaker desires. Keep your money in a glass jar and add it up at the end of the month.

3. Write without fail. Okay, so you've shown up to write and you have a blank page. Your outline isn't working, and you can't decide on a topic. All of this is normal. I usually need a few minutes before writing to get serious about what I am working on.

I start with free writing, which can be random thoughts in Word or my notebook. You don't have to publish or edit these words. They are for your eyes only. But the key is to start writing something. It's like working out at the gym.

You can't just walk in and start lifting the heavy weights before you warm up. It's best to do some stretching and ease into it. If you know what you want to write about, go for it. But take the first five minutes to warm up. This will get things moving. I rarely have a day that I'm unable to write if I do this first.

Once you are ready and the ideas are clicking, pull out your mind map or outline and get to work. You can sprint for thirty-minute increments or less. I usually go for sixty minutes and then take a five-minute break.

In two sessions, I can get an average of two thousand words written. Don't worry about the word count. We are going for habit building here. Writing is hard if you are not used to it. You need to break yourself into the habit first. After a couple of weeks, you'll be flying straight ahead.

4. Deal with resistance. This is a common obstacle that will show up and hold us back from creating. Resistance is a form of fear that latches onto the mind and pulls us off course.

If you let it, resistance will turn into a heavy form of procrastination. For years, I resisted my natural urge to write. I gave into the resistance and took the easy path—watching TV or playing games instead.

Resistance doesn't have to defeat you. As long as you follow the first two steps, you'll be fine. But getting started, even if it's just one word, can turn the momentum into a powerful snowball effect.

5. Read through your morning affirmations. Affirmations are powerful snippets of positivity that set the tone and atmosphere for writing. An affirmation could be a quote from a writer, motivational or inspiring words from someone who has been there and done that. I keep a collection of affirmations in a journal. When I'm struggling with a writing session, I'll warm up by flipping through for inspiration.

Here are some examples:

"It doesn't matter how slow you go as long as you do not stop."

— *Confucius*

"A writer who waits for ideal conditions under which to work will die without putting a word on paper."

— *E.B. White*

"Have the courage to follow your heart and intuition. They somehow know what you truly want to become."

— *Steve Jobs*

"It is impossible to live without failing at something, unless you live so cautiously that you might as well not have lived at all, in which case you have failed by default."

— J.K. Rowling

"I always wrote. I wrote from when I was 12. That was therapeutic for me in those days. I wrote things to get them out of feeling them, and onto paper. So writing in a way saved me, kept me company. I did the traditional thing with falling in love with words, reading books and underlining lines I liked and words I didn't know."

— Carrie Fisher

If you're feeling stuck, here's what you can do to get **unstuck**.

Write a sentence that is related to your topic. This can be an opening statement or the beginning of a paragraph. Just one sentence. The problem is, we spend far more time thinking about writing than actually writing. But thinking and doing are two different things. You can think about what you are going to write, but then it's time to do it. So start with a basic sentence.

6. Decide the target goal. There are two ways to decide your goals for the day. One is to write according to a predetermined length of time; the other way is by word count. I prefer the word count method because it is easier to track the words I am writing. But if you're pressed for time, you can write for just twenty or thirty minutes. Something is better than nothing.

Be sure to set everything up with clear intention. Momentum is key. If you show up at the same time with your tools ready to go, there is no reason you shouldn't be able to pound out five hundred or even one thousand words in an hour.

You can do this. You now have ten mini-strategies for starting your book. The fears of rejection are being stamped out as you continue on an incredible journey to becoming a published author. I know there is a long road ahead, but as long as you work at this every day, you'll get through it.

Get Your Writing Done

"Exercise the writing muscle every day, even if it is only a letter, notes, a title list, a character sketch, a journal entry. Writers are like dancers, like athletes. Without that exercise, the muscles seize up."

— Jane Yolen

Writers have a lot of uncertainty, and that includes the best of us. One of the biggest relates to the writing process. But if you implement this habit now, your fears of writing will be taken care of within a few months when you're polishing your book for publication.

Writing isn't easy. There are times when it can be fun, especially if you get into a state of mind where you lose yourself in the creative process. But there will be days when you show up to write your best work and instead sit numbly staring at a blank screen. Frustrated, you'll walk away. That could turn into a few days and then a few weeks.

This is why I'd like to introduce you to several well-known writing strategies. There are no magical tricks here or anything earth-shattering that you couldn't figure out on your own, but having a set of strategies ready to pull out of your pocket when things don't go according to plan can be the push you need to get your book moving.

Remember: two thousand words written in a day, about one and a half hours of writing on average, means you could be done your book in less than three weeks. When I finally set up my writing habit, I was finishing books and getting them published. The consistency of the habit works.

If you're struggling with the writing process, you've undoubtedly discovered that keeping the momentum of writing every day is tough. We start for a couple of days, take a day off, do it again the next day, and then take a week off.

Doing anything with any kind of consistency is tough—working out, saving money, and yes, writing every day.

I spent a good part of my life putting things off and chasing things that materialized into nothing. Waiting for tomorrow and always talking about the book I was going to write didn't make it happen.

What I needed was a simple system that broke this chain of procrastination. Or better yet, started a chain of consistent action. If not, I'd be wishing for that book to get written well into my senior years—and I'm not quite there yet!

The Writing Habit

By now you've no doubt heard of the one habit that writers need above all else. It isn't their skills in marketing or being able to build an effective email list with high conversion. This comes later. What makes a big difference is the writing habit you will develop to finish your book.

The writing habit is the one defense you will need to use when you don't feel like writing. If you implement the habit now, you can get through the worst of times when your mind shuts off and decides you've had enough.

A writing habit keeps you on track. It is the one guarantee that your book will get finished on time. The best part is, you won't have to worry about writer's block or the fear of not being able to write. When writing becomes a habit, it's no different than getting up and going to work in the morning.

Writing can become a habit, but first you'll hit a lot of resistance before it starts to work. I'll share my process and how I set up the writing schedule so that I consistently get three thousand words done per day. Now, if the average e-book is around 30,000 words, that's a book I am writing every ten days. Yes, that's right—every two weeks, if I take weekends off, I can get a book written. But it has to be a habit first.

In this book, there are a lot of negative factors we consider: rejection as an author, uncertainty as a creative, self-doubt, lack of motivation and the fear of failure. These attack our skills, not only what we write but how we appear to the world.

Have you gone pro yet, or are you still waiting for permission? Do you want to be a writer who published a book, or will you be talking to people years from now about the book you almost finished?

Here's how you can set yourself up with the writing habit starting today.

An Easy Plan: Make Writing a Habit

Know what you are going to write. It doesn't matter whether you have an outline for a book, an idea for a book, or you want to write about your mother's recipe for homemade cookies. We are focusing on the habit right now, and the content can come later.

If you have the outline for your book already done, that is fantastic. Use it and start to write your material, even if the outline isn't completely finished. It will evolve as the book moves along. If you show up without a game plan for writing, you'll sit there for a few minutes and then start to drift by doing other things.

Know how much you are going to write. You should decide the length of time you can commit to the writing practice. Not everyone can sit for hours and write like Stephen King. If you are new to writing and you try to do too much at once, you'll burn out and dread the writing process.

If you are just starting out, shoot for three hundred words the first day, four hundred the next. Build up to one thousand words a day and do it in one-hundred word increments. It took me about three months to build up to three thousand words a day. Now I can maintain that goal, but in the beginning when I tried it, I rarely succeeded.

Show Up with a Plan

This sounds like an obvious idea, but if you show up to write without any real idea what you're writing about, you'll find yourself drifting and then bouncing around looking for something else to do.

In order for writing to be effective, we need to have direction and a plan. This may not sound creative, but when you take the time to plan what you'll write for that session, it does make the creativity easier.

Getting into the flow of writing can only be accomplished when you have a starting point. For example, I have an outline for all the books I'm writing. From that outline, I will choose the chapter or part of the chapter I will write. This way, when I show up to write, I never ask myself what I'll write that day. If you are showing up asking yourself this question, you could be starting down the rabbit hole to nowhere.

Of course, some people can do this and just show up without any plan. You may or may not be one of them, but this plan may fail on those days you don't want to write. Those days will come. It's like any job, really. Some days you're into it, and other days you aren't.

What time are you writing?

Everyone has that time of day that is the most productive for them. While many say that the morning is the best time, it's up to your body clock. If you have always gone to bed early and you enjoy waking up before the sun rises, the morning routine would work best for you. My best time is from nine p.m. to eleven, after the family goes to bed. Everything is quiet and it works in my favor. Find what works best for you.

Now, lock it in.

Protect your writing time like you'd protect anything you hold of great value. Your phone might ring, you might receive desktop notifications, or maybe the dog wants to go for a walk and he isn't waiting. Distractions will try to pull you away from the habit.

Once you lose focus, it takes twice as long and double the energy to return to that streamlined focus. Take the dog for a walk before you write. Turn off your phone—maybe even turn off the Wi-Fi. The world won't end and you'll write two thousand words if you can keep going for two hours. Lock in your time and keep it.

Take breaks.

It's hard to sit for one or two hours straight. Get up and move around. Walk, exercise, or grab a drink—of coffee or water, that is. Stretch out. You might even be at a standing desk and need to actually sit for ten minutes. Don't make this a torture session.

If you want to go longer and work for an hour, take a ten-minute rest and begin again. But whatever system you choose, make it consistent so that your body and mind can adjust and get used to the routine.

Mark it on your calendar.

As you may already know, Jerry Seinfeld is a comedian who co-created (with Larry David) the long-standing sitcom that earned him millions.

In order to do this, Seinfeld used a strategy that built consistency into his work and he was able to create joke after joke by committing himself to taking action every day. He called it the "Don't Break the Chain" method

Jerry Seinfeld had a system for tracking his writing. He didn't become successful from talent alone. He dedicated each day to writing jokes and comedy, and when he did, he marked it on the calendar with an X. Done. He'd keep the calendar visible, and at the end of the week or month, he could see the progress he made with keeping the habit.

It works like this. Get yourself a wall calendar—the bigger, the better. Then, for every day that you write, put a big X on that day. The goal is not to break the chain.

Seinfeld did this every day so he could keep writing consistently. He said it didn't matter if the jokes were bad. In fact, most of them were—by his own admission. But by creating a strategic action plan of sitting down every day and writing jokes, he got funnier.

When you're kicking yourself for not getting any writing done, just look at the calendar and visualize all those Xs running through it. That's you writing your book. See how many you can get in a row before the chain is broken. If you do break it, don't beat yourself up. Count the days you were consistent.

For example, I have a writing target of one thousand words a day. That's my bottom line target. If I have a chain of ten days on my calendar, it means I wrote ten thousand words. That's not bad. You can even write your word count on the calendar so you can track how many words you've actually written.

Remember, good writing comes with building a habit of consistency. If you do something often enough, you'll get better at it. With that comes greater confidence. Will you be worth $800 million dollars someday from your writing? I don't know, but at least you'll finish your book!

Get Over the Fear of Shipping

"Shipping is fraught with risk and danger. Every time you raise your hand, send an email, launch a product or make a suggestion, you're exposing yourself to criticism. Not just criticism, but the negative consequences that come with wasting money, annoying someone in power or making a fool of yourself. It's no wonder we're afraid to ship."

— Seth Godin

If you're reading this, you've finished your first draft and it's time to get down to editing. But wait...your thinking about taking a break?

I had an author tell me once that finalizing their book, being able to say, "it's finished," and shipping it to an editor was the equivalent to sending a child off to college. For the first time in the child's life, they will be on their own to face the perils of the universe without Mom and Dad. Letting your book go and having someone else read and critique it is a daunting step. This is another obstacle that causes procrastination and triggers feelings of rejection.

"What if the editor hates it?"

"What if they tell me to rewrite the whole thing?"

"What if it confirms my worst fears that I'm really bad at writing?"

The fears of finishing your book are endless.

If you are struggling with letting your book go, as many new authors are, here are the reasons why we must let it fly.

I once heard that a writer is someone who publishes books. As a self-published author, you are not just writing a book, but you are responsible for getting it to print, marketing the book, and building future sales.

Six reasons to publish your book

1. An unpublished book doesn't make money.

It costs on average $1,200 to write, publish, and market your self-published book. This could be a lot less for you or a lot more depending on your budget. At the very least, we want to make our money back. But a book can only make cash if it's a finished product. Yes, you already know this, but think about it: When you publish your book, you have the potential to make money every day that adds up to monthly revenue.

2. If you set it aside to finish later, you'll never come back to it.

Procrastination is rampant. It's hard enough to show up every day to write, but can you imagine what happens when you set your book aside for a few days to cool? My advice is to set it aside for one day and then get right into the self-edit.

Be tough on yourself with this rule. If you let it go more than a week, you're risking not getting back to it. I have seen this happen plenty of times in coaching authors and with my own books. Out of sight and out of mind is what happens when you walk away from it for too long.

3. An unpublished book won't build your list.

Gathering email lists is a powerful way to grow your business and build community. But this can only happen if you have something to offer people. In this case, your book is the calling card that opens doors.

Your book is the gateway to a new way of life. With it you can build a business from the ground up, offer it to new customers and clients in your current business, or gather emails to spread the word about your next book or educational course.

4. An unpublished book is unforgiving.

I set aside my first book for a "break" after finishing the first draft. That was a mistake. I then "forgot" about it for six months. It stayed on my desktop as this glaring unfinished project. I don't know about you, but an incomplete project is like a monkey on your back that sticks until you can shake it off. You have to finish your book no matter what. Unfinished books are very unforgiving, at least for me. For months, I carried guilt around wherever I went, as if the unfinished book was begging to be set free. If you don't finish it, you'll never let yourself down. Do you want that guilt?

5. Telling people, "I'm writing a book," isn't nearly as convincing as showing them what you've got.

For years, I was writing a book. Even when I wasn't writing I would tell people about my aspirations. But no one is impressed by your imagination or what you are going to do. They want to see what you've got and what you have accomplished. A finished product is something you can show people and not just tell them about. Imagine meeting someone on the street for the first time. When they ask what you do, you can reach into your bag and pull out a copy of your latest book. It's a great feeling to know you finished your book. For many writers, this was the dream moment of their life. Will it be yours?

6. A published book can change everything.

Books are powerful when they reach the right people. Your fans and supporters will share it on social media. You can build your list. Opportunities that didn't exist before will soon be knocking on your door—podcast interviews, new friendships, and if things go really well, maybe a book contract.

The point is, you have no idea what could happen when you hit publish and your book gains traction. There is a transition period from finishing a first draft to starting the editing process. This is the part of the book process that trips everyone up. We finished, so we want to rest, take it easy and relax for a while. But now is the time to push even harder than ever.

Why is shipping fearful?

There is a greater risk in not finishing your book. You'll make mistakes on your publishing journey and you can recover from them, but the worst mistake is not taking any action at all.

Do you want to publish or not?

If you do, then it's time to finish self-editing the book and send it to your editor.

Done Is Better Than Perfect

"Our most powerful writing comes from the subconscious, that part of the brain we access when we shut down that inner critic and just let the words come. Fear of judgment will shut that part down, and we have to learn to let it go. Yes, it's a risk, but it's the only way your work will sing."

— Joanna Penn, *The Successful Author Mindset*

Six Strategies to Prepare You for Publication

I have heard many people say, "I'll publish when the book is perfect."

I know the temptation. We want a book that's flawless and will sell a thousand copies the first day. Let me share a secret with you. If you wait until your book is perfect, it'll never get published and you won't sell anything. An unpublished book makes zero sales. A book that is good (not perfect) gets into the hands of readers and could inspire change.

So let's abandon our perfectionist ideas for the moment. They won't work if you want to publish.

There are five rules I have about editing.

1. Let yourself breathe. When I self-edit, I beat myself up about how bad the writing is. Well, it's supposed to be bad. This is a first draft. You have permission to clean up your flawed book. That's what a first draft is. Give yourself credit for making it to this milestone. Remember that only one percent of those who want to write a book ever do. You are writing it and you're almost halfway there. Give yourself a pat on the back and a reward. You are doing this!

2. Do not let the editing process take more than two weeks. In my experience, most authors get caught up in self-editing. I've seen it take years. I've seen people abandon their books entirely out of frustration. Others took months to do complete rewrites. Then, another rewrite after that. We want our books to be of the best quality, of course. I am not suggesting you just change a few words and be done with it. But on the other hand, you don't want this to take six months either.

The longer you spend on self-editing, the less your patience will stand the test of time. You'll reach a point of frustration that happens to most and set it aside to cool down. This is your brain's way of saying, "I've had enough. I'll finish it later."

Later never comes. We get busy with other things and forget about our books. So, make a promise to yourself to get this done within two weeks. It's a tight schedule, but you can do it.

3. Contact and hire your editor at the beginning of the editing process. You want to have your editor lined up and ready to go. This is the intimidating part. If it's your first time hiring an editor, you might feel resistant to the idea. You're going to pay someone to read, critique, and make loads of comments about your writing style.

This is good stuff. That part I said about your book not being perfect? Well, your editor is going to make it as perfect as possible. But you need to hire them before you start the self-edit. Then, as soon as you are ready, it can be sent to the editor.

4. Don't put your manuscript aside. Many writers think they need to put their book aside to take a nap for a few days. This is open to debate and there is no right or wrong. Set it aside for a week and you can return to it with a fresh mind. But let it sit for too long and you could get distracted with another project, forgetting that you have a book to finish. I know many writers who fell into this trap and set aside their book to take a break. That break can last months.

By the time they returned to it, they had all but forgotten the purpose of the book. If you set it aside, give yourself reminders to pick it up on a specific date. Don't just think you'll get back to it when you feel like it. That's a danger sign for procrastination. Believe me, once you start to put something off, it gets easier each day to distance yourself from it. Stick with your plan. Set a "break date" and be firm about it.

5. Do the FINAL PROOF and let it go. When that book is back from the editor, it's time to give it the final touches. There are several ways to do this. You can set up a team of beta readers to proof it before its launch. This is a great idea.

There are people hanging out on Facebook groups, or in your mastermind circle if you have one, who might be willing to read it. Post it in your circle and see. If not, you can hire someone through Upwork or Freelancer.

Many professional proofreaders can be found here. Prices vary, so you'll want to check around, but I encourage you to pay for quality. Check out the freelancer's profile before you decide. Do they have a substantial amount of reviews? How is the rating overall? Take time to really probe each candidate and you can even send them a sample of your work to try them out.

6. Be the writer you deserve to be. I didn't write anything for years because I was afraid of finding out that I wasn't a good writer. I was afraid of discovering my writing was bad instead of good. I talked about writing, read books on the subject, and read the kinds of books I wanted to write. But I didn't write anything. I had lofty dreams of accomplishing something, but never actually set out to do it.

This is the difference between reading about a great place you'd like to visit and actually taking the journey. You can only overcome perfectionist tendencies if you take that first step.

You can always rearrange things later and make it better. You can always go back and make changes. But you can only do this if you've completed a book to begin with.

We try to be perfect because we're afraid we might let ourselves down. We fear failure. It was easier—albeit unrealistic—to dream about success rather than make it happen. I've been there. The perfection game is the first big failure people encounter and they don't realize it until the end.

Punch Out Your Inner Critic

"Rejection slips, or form letters, however tactfully phrased, are lacerations of the soul, if not quite inventions of the devil— but there is no way around them."

— Isaac Asimov

In this chapter, I am going to dive into perfection on a deeper scale. If perfection is one of your roadblocks, by the time you're finished reading this chapter, it will be a thing of the past.

I could write an entire book around the power of perfection and how it destroys dreams. But we don't need a book for that. According to a survey, approximately sixty-seven percent of the American population copes with some form of perfectionism.

This could involve trying to be a good parent, employee, or be the most perfect version of oneself possible. For the author or artist, it is to create the perfect masterpiece that changes the world.

First off, let me start by saying that perfection is an illusion. It is and always has been. Nothing in the universe is perfect, except for the universe itself. If you are smaller than the universe, you are imperfect, and that's totally okay.

Editing doesn't have to be a complicated process. In fact, it is quite easy if you use the system I propose in the following chapters. But what makes it complicated is the internal critic we all have in our minds. This critic won't let you be, but it demands perfection, and what better way to get it than when you write a book.

A good friend of mine once said, "If you are not careful, the committee of voices in your head will run the show." That's what we have here. A committee of voices born from past events and living out their lives in your mind. When it comes to criticism, most people are hard on themselves. This isn't just a problem that writers have, but writing a book is what we are doing, so let's keep it simple.

During the writing phase, we decided we're not going to edit while we write. I know this is a lot to ask, but now that you are through the first draft, I hope you can see the reason why. While we are writing, the brain is tapped into the left side where your creativity exists.

On the right side is the analytical part of the brain that is designed for editing. Trying to use both at the same time is like running a machine in forward and reverse at once. We don't want to do that. It slows everything down.

Now that your first draft is done, it's time to edit the book.

For most authors, this is the hardest part of the process. You are going to cut, paste, fix and clean up your manuscript. Stephen King said, "Kill your darlings, kill your darlings, even when it breaks your egocentric little scribbler's heart, kill your darlings."

Real writing is about rewriting. The first draft is the foundation for the book. The editing involves working with the real structure.

But editing has several stages. You may be wondering why I am covering editing in this book. By now you've realized that writing can be both an adventure and a slow death.

We struggle with many varying emotions in this stage. Rejection, doubt, happiness, and anxiety. Criticism is the one thing that will kill your creativity in a moment. And when it comes to our writing, nobody is harder on it than you.

Before we get into editing, I'll dive into the elements of your inner critic and why it's so important that you confront this monster from the beginning.

Criticism is a license to label someone or something based on our own worldview and perception. Think of a time when you criticized someone else for something they did. Chances are you felt justified in your anger or judgment. They hurt you or did something that provoked your disapproval. In your justification you labeled, condemned, and stamped your opinion on that person or incident. And that was that.

But what about the other person? What is their story? Whatever it is they did, did they deserve your criticism? If you were to ask them, I'm sure they would disagree and defend their right to be themselves.

Kill the Internal Critic

When it comes to writing, we struggle with this critic. But now, instead of attacking someone else, we are the target. Instead of feeling powerful and righteous, our own self-critic is pounding us down. Our inner critic is powerful and delivers painful words that scorn.

This is something many writers deal with.

But it doesn't have to defeat you. And it won't. I promise.

Criticism, especially self-criticism, is nothing but an illusion.

My aim here is to give you the basics for dealing with your inner critic and putting it to rest for good. You don't have to fear writing when you are a writer.

Feeling like "this suck and so do I" is a very common experience for writers. Sure, we can write up a first draft, but then we have to face what's on the page, and it is one of the biggest obstacles of the journey. If you get over this, you'll get your book written. You can also stop criticizing yourself for being a bad writer.

Recognize when your thoughts are running you down. You can shut down your internal negativity when you catch it lashing out at you. Talk back to the voice that is trying to overpower your mind. It gets its power when you believe what you are listening to internally. Bring in the writer who has driven you this far.

Tell yourself, "I believe that I am going to get this book written, no matter what!" Your positive affirmations are therapy for removing internal criticism. You can also listen to your thoughts as they are happening. Don't try to control them. Let these thoughts pass through. Listen to music or read a passage from a book that empowers you.

Working Through the 2nd Rewrite

"The world breaks everyone and afterward many are strong at the broken places."

— **Ernest Hemingway**, *A Farewell to Arms*

Now that we have taken a look at the inner critic and how you can best deal with that, it is time to rewrite your book if you have finished. For the sake of this book, I am using the terms "rewrite" and "revise" interchangeably.

When it comes to rewriting, we don't want this to take forever. In the old days, writers would spend a year or more rewriting their books. But that was before they had any tools, computers, or Internet.

Now, a year spent on a rewrite would be like an eternity. Trust me when I say that you don't want to be editing your book five years from now. Give yourself a limit of two weeks and push to have it ready within this timeframe. Once your book comes back from the editor and you can identify the weak sections or chapters, you have a better idea what to focus on.

The second rewrite (or revision) is the stage when your book really starts to take shape. The rewrite may happen simultaneously with the self-edit. Or it can be a separate step. I like to do the self-edit with a verbal read-through, fix and add a few things and then do the rewrite. This is the part where we can really add more depth to the book.

Starting from the introduction, read through each paragraph. Read quickly the first time. How does it sound? If there is anything out of place, or if you feel it's too thin, add more details.

If there is any repetition where you said the same thing several times already, take it out. Repetition is one of the most common issues. We don't know how to express something in just a basic sentence, so we overkill it with long-winded explanations.

If you notice anything like that, go ahead and rewrite it. If you miss anything, your editor will get it. That's their job, after all. I often hear writers say, "I'll send it in for editing as soon as I catch all the mistakes." That's why we hire people to edit. If you're paying for it, get the most out of it by letting a paid professional clean it up. This gives us more time to work on the launch.

During the second rewrite, read through each paragraph as if you are reading out loud to someone (and maybe you are). You want the book to flow and have a logical order. Cut anything that's fluff or has no value.

Yes, cutting your words away is painful, but you want every word to have a place on your page. Readers don't want fluff. They want transformation and valuable information. Give them what they want, and you'll have a winner.

Taking Feedback from Your Editor

Your editor is probably the first person who will see your manuscript. You may have let some friends or family members read through it and they gave you a thumbs up, but the editor's job isn't to boost your confidence and tell you how great your writing is.

They will (and should) give you the no-holds-barred truth about what needs to be fixed. This can be hard to take if you are sensitive to criticism, and many people are. So, what do you do if you get your manuscript back and it has more red marks on it than white space?

Simple. You take it as constructive feedback and get to work. Maybe that isn't the answer you wanted to hear, but there are two choices. You can question the corrections your editor has made, and in some cases, challenge them. Or, you can work through your manuscript line by line, accepting the corrections as you move through the book, making additions here and there.

The second option is easier. Remember why we hire editors in the first place: to make our books the best they can be. You can't edit your own manuscript. That is not even an option. Your editor is the one person who is helping you bring this book to life.

If you think they have harsh statements about your work, what do you think will happen when this book is available to the general public? The way I deal with editorial comments is simple. It's better to hear it now behind closed doors than later in a bad review from an angry reader who claims the book is flawed. I don't always agree with suggestions made by my editor, but rest assured, they can see the things we can't.

If you aren't sure, you can always ask someone else, preferably an accountability partner, for a second opinion. I would avoid asking family members unless you know they can give you a very unbiased opinion.

Catching errors now is better than having readers catch them after they paid for your book. Trust me, I've been there, and I can tell you firsthand that it's better to make it great now instead of later.

So, when it comes time to work through your editing, stick with your editor's suggestions. Run through the book page-by-page, paragraph-by-paragraph, and line-by-line. Read it as if you are reading it for the first time.

Then, make the corrections as suggested by your editor, and rewrite any sections based on their advice. The editing process can be one of the longest [and difficult] parts of writing. But it is here that you really grasp what writing is about. During the editing stage, you can work through your fears and doubts. You can overcome the resistance to hold on to your work and ship it out to the world where it has influence.

Bad Reviews, Naysayers, and the Critics

"The only thing I was fit for was to be a writer, and this notion rested solely on my suspicion that I would never be fit for real work, and that writing didn't require any."

— Russell Baker

Let's be honest. We hate criticism. Sure, we talk about how much it makes us grow and become better people, but the bottom line is, we want people to love us. When you get a bad review, or someone mentions on social media that they didn't like your book, it can crush your confidence. And, of course, it lends to fears of rejection. You might think your writing is no good.

The fear of criticism can stall your writing habit and prevent you from publishing. In this section, we'll tackle the hardest part of the business for authors. Handling criticism, public speaking, social branding, and reaching out to influencers. This is your chance to light up your craft and develop skills for putting yourself out there. In fact, the authors who can take it on the chin are those most likely to survive through the toughest battles with criticism.

Unfortunately, this just isn't the case in the real world. Regardless of whether you're an author, artist or musician, when you put your work out there it's going to be judged, critiqued, and put to the test. Some will love it, others will accept it, and another group will tear it up.

This is the part of the business that will toughen you up. It is one thing to have people on a launch team who "know" you and are willing to support your book when it launches. You can be confident that the reviews and feedback you get are positive (almost always) and that everyone on the team is a trusted member looking to spread the word about your book to help drive sales and turn it into a bestseller.

But we have to be realistic. Bad reviews are inevitable. If you are sensitive (who isn't?) a bad review on your book can sting. I know of one author who even removed her book from Amazon because of one damaging review.

Rejection is like sitting on a hot seat.

Nobody wants to get burned.

In this chapter, I'm going to put your fears to rest about getting bad reviews. We do have to drink a cup of reality. You are in the spotlight when your book is available to be purchased and read by millions of people. If you can't accept that some readers are not going to enjoy your work and that they may express their opinion publicly, you might want to consider a different line of work.

You're still here? Okay, great.

First of all, there are three types of reviewers who will leave a negative review.

The first type is the constructive critic. This is, in my opinion, the type of negative review that is useful. This is a reader who actually read your book, maybe enjoyed parts of it, but didn't feel that it warranted anything more than two stars. If you're lucky, they took the time to tell you why they didn't like it.

I take these reviews seriously because it points out potential flaws in the manuscript that I didn't notice before. When I see reviews like this, I pay attention. These reviewers are doing you a favor by telling you how to make the book better.

The Negative Critic

This type of reviewer isn't as kind. Maybe they read the book, but they aren't taking the time to leave you any comments. Their review might say, "It was okay," or even, "This is garbage," and they might have given you one star or perhaps two. This isn't helping you as an author and can be a kick to your ego, but it happens to most people.

There's another way to look at this. If you have twenty positive reviews and a few negative reviews, it's a good balance. You are doing something right. Unless your book is a major game changer that is loved by millions, I'd expect a few negatives and be done with it. You can choose to respond or not.

The Troll Critic

These are the reviews we fear the most. Trolls drop reviews without reading the book or understating what it's about. If you check their Amazon review profile, they've undoubtedly left similar reviews for other people. I would not respond to a troll.

However, if you think the review is unjustified or is character-damaging, contact Amazon Customer Support and they will review your case. There's a good chance they will remove the review if it is a comment unrelated to the content of the book or threatens to damage your reputation somehow.

Having said that, keep in mind a negative review doesn't necessarily mean someone is out to get you. Most reviews are legitimate and readers have the right to express their opinion. If you get a bad review that says "boring" or "not worth my time," that's just the way it is.

You can comment in a professional manner and offer to refund the reader's money if you like, but if not, let it be. Instead, focus on improving your writing. Make it so good that people will be asking for more. If they love what you do, they'll be waiting for your next book or blog post. If not, they won't.

Reviews are critical to your book's success. If you're nervous about having others read and judge your work, this is the part of the business that can toughen you up. You might experience rejection or critical shame when someone dislikes or even hates it, but remember that even bestselling books have multiple negative reviews. This comes with the territory. The best you can do is develop a thick skin and a strategy for dealing with it.

Tips on Handling Negative Reviews

First of all, don't be distraught. We can learn from this. Even if ten percent of your readers don't approve of your work, a large percentage is still getting something out of it and finding value in what you do.

1. Learn from the review. Read what the customer is telling you. If they didn't like a certain part of the book, and they were good enough to tell you why, go back to that section and see if it can be improved. Pay particular attention if you receive several reviews saying the same thing. There is obviously a problem you missed.

Having said that, it's imperative that your book is up to quality standards. This means it has to be edited, formatted, and professional in appearance. If it's not, you can expect a higher negative review response.

For example, I've seen some books with a seventy percent negative review rate. Why? Poor editing and formatting. The material is disorganized. We can find this out by reading the reviews. Make sure your book is up to the highest standards possible and you'll reduce the amount of negative reviews.

The key point here is to respond with love. Always with love. If you respond in a defensive tone and set up barriers for attack, it makes you look unprofessional. Follow what others do in this situation. If the review is semi-constructive, respond with a note of thanks. Mind you, this isn't for the person who leaves the review—it's to show other readers and fans that you're professional and open-minded.

2. Everyone is biased. Some people will love your work. A percentage will hate it. But why might someone dislike your book? We can take this as a personal attack on our creative genius, but it really isn't. Readers expect your work to help them. If it doesn't, they may respond negatively. That's it.

Most people who leave less-than-positive reviews did so because they were expecting something from your book that they didn't get. Sometimes the reader misunderstood what the book was about or the content disturbed them. They may have seen the cover or read the title and thought they were getting one thing, when in fact it could be the complete opposite.

3. Getting down on critics. The great thing about criticism is that it really does build you up for taking on more. In fact, if you develop a thicker skin, you are going to reach out to people in ways you never imagined. Soon you'll be signing up for interviews and chasing down podcasters to share your message. Your enthusiasm for communicating will draw the attention of those who want to hear what you have to say.

If you are receiving criticism for something you wrote, that's a good thing. In what world is an artist *not* under some kind of conflict, criticism, or strife? It comes with the territory. People will love you or they'll hate you. It isn't always about you, either. You may have written something that hit an emotional chord with someone and they reacted based on their emotions. They might strike out against you on social media or send you a direct message.

Here's how I deal with critics. Respond if you must, but keep in mind that you are a professional author. Professionals need to remain vigilant even in the line of fire. If you start an argument with someone online or even in person, it escalates as you both make attempts to get your point across. People will have opinions. Let it be. Let them have their day. You are too busy writing the next book to get into a debate.

The critics are fans, too.

An author friend of mine said that he gets email from at least two people a week who don't like his work. Some of them even go into long rants. He said that when this first started, it really bothered him. He would fire back at the critics and invite them to engage in an all-out battle. But he found he was spending more time worrying, engaging in confrontation, and defending his work than actually creating new content.

It occurred to him that if these people were taking the time to write emails and go out of their way to give him a message about how his work stirred them up, wouldn't they be his fans as well? Why do fans have to be just people who love you? Don't they have personalities of their own? Can't they derail you as easily as they might help you? Instead of replying in anger to the criticism, he started thanking these people for their thoughts. Once that was done, the critics who were looking for a fight had nothing left to say.

So if someone publicly states that your book or creative work is crap and they want nothing to do with it, so be it. If you still have a seventy percent positivity rate, that's a good thing, isn't it? What if it's sixty or only fifty percent? Still good. Half the people like you, and the other half who don't still know who you are and they might be swayed by your next book.

Handling Critical Feedback

Criticism is something we don't always enjoy, but we can appreciate that people are providing us with legitimate feedback to improve our craft. My best work is created when I ask people for honest feedback on what I have written. It may be hard to take, but remember that it's about your readers and not you, the author.

Think of yourself as a funnel that creates material people need to either learn or be entertained by. Without your commitment to this work, they may not find that particular fulfillment they seek. To get there, you have to get used to the constructive feedback that is only there to help you.

Battling against yourself just leads to frustration and you might even give up to avoid any more rejection.

In a perfect world, everyone loves our work, loves us and thinks that everything we do is fantastic.

In a perfect world.

But this isn't a perfect world.

People will love you, support you, and cheer you on. Others won't like what you do, disagree with your statements or opinions, and might even insult you on social media. Books get bad reviews and you could end up defending yourself for something you said in your book or in a recent interview.

It happens.

When you become a writer or content creator, you are in constant contact with people from all over the world. This is no longer a closed community. The world is our stage and we are here to dance. The image of a writer locked up in a cabin isolated from the world is a fairy tale that we long for, but in reality, we are dancing on stage every day, practicing our craft, making mistakes and learning how to laugh when things go wrong.

Respond with professional courtesy to negative feedback. It makes you all the better for it.

So, what you can do is:

- Thank the reviewer for their feedback.

- Offer to provide something for free to compensate the reviewer.

- Avoid defensive remarks.

- Move on.

The Fearless Approach to Marketing Your Book

"There are three rules for writing a novel. Unfortunately, no one knows what they are."

— W. Somerset Maugham

There are so many ways to market a book and yourself as an author that it deserves its own podcast or series of books. Marketing is the most effective tool authors have. It is also the critical area in which most authors do poorly. And this is myself included.

I used to be a poor marketer. Not a natural salesman when it came to promoting my work, I froze up. Again, it was those voices of doubt. What if people don't like me? What if I say something stupid? What if I make a mistake and look like an amateur? Yes, all these things can and probably will happen.

The other option is to play it safe and do nothing. No marketing and hence no action. But we want to flourish, right? After all, what's the point if nobody reads our stuff or listens to the message we're trying to convey?

Your comfort zone as an author is a hazardous place to be in. I say this from experience. Most authors I know are afraid to put themselves out there. They don't believe they are experts, or they think because they don't have a PhD or some high-end qualification that nobody will take them seriously.

But the reverse is true. You see, it isn't the world that needs to change its perspective. It is you. If you're worried about the crowd not taking you seriously, it's because you aren't taking yourself seriously. Do you believe or not? Are you a writer or not? Will you publish a series of books or not? Are you good enough to be featured on Oprah or not? If you've made it through the writing and editing phases and you thought it was tough, I have some good news for you. The fun is really going to begin now.

Up until now we have been struggling with and working through our own personal views about perfection, rejection, and self-esteem. You may have come to realize that all the fear was in your head. It always has been. But now we are getting our book ready for the market. This means scrutiny. People forming opinions. Judgments. Yes, everything we try to avoid on a daily basis at work, at home, or in public.

Now we are going to cover the strategies for dealing with rejection from the crowd. This can be more terrifying than dealing with it when you're alone in your room trying to write a book. But don't worry. I've got your back here. Having dealt with public rejection, scrutiny, and judgment many times, I can tell you that you'll survive no matter what happens.

If you are ready, it's time to start taking your book to market. This means getting the word out there and telling people who you are and what it is you do. More importantly, why your work is so important and what it can do to help them.

4 Fears Authors Have When Talking About Their Books

1. Responsibility. What if someone asks you for more advanced information that you aren't prepared to provide? This was always a fear of mine. I avoided doing interviews for the longest time because I didn't want to be asked something I couldn't answer. What if I looked stupid? What if I wasn't the authority they thought I was? What if they expected more from me?

When you write a book, whether it's fiction or nonfiction, there is a certain level of responsibility that comes with it. People now look to you for answers. You've proven your authority by writing a book. Now you may be expected to take it to the next level. But responsibility builds character. It creates fortitude. It expands your options.

The more reliable you become for others, the more you are in a position to help them. For years, I wanted to avoid the spotlight. As I published more books and people took a real interest, my fear dissipated. I could see the opportunity this was creating. When I spoke, somebody listened.

When I wrote a book, there were readers who wanted what I had created because it helped them with something. What I experienced was a sense of empowerment. The responsibility of living up to my own expectations were frightening. But the reality of staying stuck and not taking this to the next level scared me more.

2. Authority. One of the fears that has always held me back is a fear that I wouldn't be recognized as an authority of any sort. After all, real authority figures have a knack for public speaking. They know their trade and can fire back when under pressure. But what constitutes authority isn't how much you know or how much success you've had. There are always new heights of success to aim for and if you wait until you achieve a certain status, you may never get there.

If I have an interview or a coaching session with a customer, I plant the idea in my mind that I am good enough to be the authority. Maybe I don't have all the answers, but who does? Being an authority is having the willingness to help others and the desire to grow as an author, entrepreneur, or whatever else you're working toward.

3. Technology. Another big one that stumps a lot of writers is the vast amount of technology we have today. The amount of software, educational courses, and tools available to us is mind-blowing and leaves us with no boundaries. You're limitless when it comes to the power of marketing products and yourself. But this technology isn't always easy to navigate.

For example, many of the tools we should consider familiarizing ourselves with include:

- Creating landing pages

- Website design

- Setting up your email capturing system so you can build a list

- Writing software such as Scrivener

- DIY book covers and formatting

- Navigating the many features of Facebook

- Utilizing various social media platforms for promotion, marketing, and communicating

- Apps to manage your writing projects

There is so much we can do these days that has made our self-publishing options limitless, easier, and highly impactful. The downside is that it compounds the amount of information and skills we may need to adopt to take our writing to the next levels.

For many people, this sudden access to technology leaves them feeling left behind. Because there seems to be a new app or course every other week, it can lead to confusion about what to really focus on. We should adopt the mindset that the technology available to us as writers can greatly enhance what is possible. Don't feel pressured to do everything. Learning curves happen over time. Learn what you need to do to get the job done and move on.

4. Bulletproof Marketing Approach. I'm going to go out on a limb and say that marketing has always been my weakest link. Promoting my work and telling the world that I have something to say has been the biggest struggle to get through.

I am a writer, not a marketer or salesperson.

At least, that's what I thought.

I was wrong.

As a self-published author, you are in business for yourself from day one. You don't work for Amazon Kindle or iBooks; you work for yourself. And unless you have thousands to throw down on a marketing team, you are going to have to get tough with your marketing tactics.

I won't lie. This is and can be very intimidating. Shooting a video of yourself talking about your book. Signing up for a webinar or hosting one about your work and your message. Asking bloggers if you can guest post on their site.

For the longest time, I stayed hidden behind my books. I thought just posting on Facebook was marketing, or the occasional Tweet about what I was launching. That isn't marketing. If you want to market your work, you need to find your audience and market to them. Go straight for the gold.

This is frightening, and if you struggle with rejection, doubt, or lack confidence, marketing yourself as a professional author is the best way to overcome it. In fact, it is the cure to everything. For the longest time, I admired entrepreneurs who could just get behind a camera or a microphone and tell everyone who they were and what they did. People who do interviews, shoot video, and put themselves out there are displaying acts of courage and trust in their brand.

We could do this as well.

Now I am going to cover six strategies for marketing your next bestselling book. This will break any fears you have about rejection or the fear of being seen.

These strategies are ways to get you out of your comfort zone. While connecting with people on social media is one form of communication, it won't be nearly as effective as taking advantage of the ideas below. If you want to break your fear of public speaking, you have to get on stage or put yourself in front of people with your image or voice. Show them you are a real person.

Six Ways to Capture Readers

1. Podcast Interviews. Podcast interviews are a great way to reach a large audience. Not only that, but doing interviews gives readers an inside look into who you are as a person. This can drive book sales. More importantly, if your fear is putting yourself out there, interviews will help toughen you up.

You will reach a wider audience, and it adds greater credibility to your brand and empowers you as an authority on the topic you write about. Writing is one medium, but your voice takes it to a new level. You can reach out to the podcasters in your niche and set up several interviews per week. Most podcasts are always looking for people to share wisdom, advice, and personality.

How do you set up a podcast interview?

You can find a list of popular podcasts for writers right here. Or, if your book is in the personal development genre, do a search on Google and this will give you a list of podcasts available.

Then, contact the podcaster directly to ask if they would be interested in having you on the show.

2. Book Signings. Can you imagine showing up at a bookstore to a signing and having rows of fans line up to greet you? Well, you can do that. In fact, I can't think of a better way to get out there and connect with people than by hosting a public signing.

You could videotape the experience and have photos taken of you with readers at the signings. You can post these to your website, as well. Contact your local bookstore to see if they would be interested in setting this up for you. It could be great attention for the store as well as for you. You can also try to set up a consignment contract with the bookstore.

3. Host a Webinar. Several authors host live webinars about their books before launching, or during the launch of the book. This is a high-end strategy that can bring in serious traffic if people share the webinar and invite their traffic as well.

During the webinar, you would answer questions and invite attendees to sign up for the book launch when it is ready to be released. They would receive the book for free on launch day. You could give away free content during the webinar, such as a workbook or a sample from the book.

4. Give Away Book Copies. Order thirty to forty copies of your book through whichever printing service you are using. At the author purchase price, this could be around $150.

Then, find a busy area in town and hand your books out to random people. There is some cost to this, but it's a great strategy to get yourself out there and promote your work. You can also engage with people outside and talk to them about your content and message.

5. Use a Video Platform. Writing about something is one thing but shooting a video and talking about it is another. Video is another way that readers and fans can connect with you on a deeper level. Your audience will be able to see the face behind the book. You will appear more human to your audience and this can even turn into a webinar that takes the video to a new level.

You could create a YouTube series, a learning series including weekly strategies, or a video discussing your latest book release. The best part about video is that it breaks you out of your fear of rejection, similar to a podcast interview. It is easy to hide behind the words in a book when there isn't any interaction going on. But with video we are vulnerable and real. If you have a fear of media or public speaking, this is one way to get over that.

6. Create a Website. Not every author has a website, but serious authors do. If you want to take your business to the level it deserves, you need a website or a blog. Readers are looking for a way to connect with you and to check out what else you have to offer.

Your website is the place where you can promote your current and future books, blog about your content more in-depth, collect subscriber emails and build an email list, and publish your video and media content.

Are you wondering if you need a website? This is a personal choice, of course. Your website should be built on a self-hosted, theme-based platform so that readers can find you through your domain name.

Writing a book takes a lot of work. But the real work is in getting your book noticed, promoting it in various channels, and setting up your author brand to drive traffic and sales your way. The above strategies are highly recommended to build your business and brand. At the very least, set up your website and use it to publish new content for your fans and existing email list.

Establishing Your Author Community and Mastermind Groups

"A professional writer is an amateur who didn't quit."

— Richard Bach

There is power in numbers, and you'll find a lot of strength in hooking up with the right people. In my writing journey I've discovered the best part of the trip is meeting with and collaborating with like-minded authors.

One of the struggles with writing or creating anything, for that matter, is staying accountable to goals. For years, I worked alone without reaching out to anyone. Is it any wonder it took years to complete my first book? I know now the core reason for this is because I had no accountability. I didn't answer to anyone and there wasn't anyone checking in on how I was doing. It was a lonely existence.

If you connect with the right people, in this case authorpreneurs, you'll get through the tough spots with your writing and finish your work.

There are four reasons to have an accountability partner when writing a book.

1. You hold each other accountable to deadlines. Being held accountable for something exponentially increases your chances of finishing it. Your partner, if they stick to the plan, will be there to push you forward. Until I had accountability, I was always moving the goal posts. In fact, a deadline means very little if you can move it without anyone noticing.

When you tell your partner what your deadline is for finishing a writing project, ask them to check in with you at least once a week. Both partners benefit when they take an interest in each other's success.

2. You pick each other up during tough moments. When you get stuck, you need a push. Without that support it is easy to stay paralyzed indefinitely. During the writing phase, editing, and then launching to market, there are several holes you will fall into during which you'll need somebody to reach out to for advice, make suggestions, or do you a favor to get past the hurdle. Authors who write alone are alone. They launch without support and I have yet to see any succeed without a team standing behind to help.

3. Expand your network. When you have an accountability partner, you are opening up the doors to more opportunity. You can introduce each other to various connections, share information, and make friends on both sides.

After meeting several people through networking, I discovered my volume of friends exploded almost overnight. I went from knowing almost nobody to being included in groups that shared success stories, helped with launch teams and provided valuable feedback on products and all book related things.

4. Overcome those thick mental barriers. When I get stuck on an idea or concept I reach out to other people for their opinions or suggestions. This has allowed me to stay unstuck in many areas of the process.

When we come up against walls of self-doubt or uncertainty, talking it through with others can break the fear. I see many people get stuck because they are afraid to ask for help. What they don't realize is that the support is out there; you just have to be willing to ask for it.

5. Form unbreakable relationships. We live in amazing times. We can connect with people at any point on the earth instantly. When I was a kid, your friends were the kids in your neighborhood and that was it. But now, we can make friends all over the world.

What this means is your support circle can grow significantly and you can bond with people without ever having met them in person. I still have weekly calls with people about writing projects and brainstorming ideas even though we have never met in person.

This is how a truly successful business can be created, and you can form a business relationship with people just through communicating online. You can use Skype, Google Hangouts or Facebook Messenger. You name it, and you can do it.

If you don't have an accountability partner yet, or you haven't joined any groups, I suggest you make this step right away. But don't expect it to happen overnight. You have to be a solid participant, even if you are just starting out, and remember to add value by providing solutions or feedback to other people's questions.

In other words, get active. Update people on your writing project and start to gain buzz. Before you know it, you'll be connecting with people who share an interest in what you're working on.

ALLI [Alliance of Independent Authors]

This is a non-profit association for self-publishing authors. As stated on their site: "Our alliance offers connection and collaboration, advice and education, advocacy and representation to writers who want to self-publish well."

There are four levels of membership you can choose from: Associate, Author, Professional or Partnership. This depends on your publishing goals and the size of your platform.

This alliance has great support and connects you with authors who are regularly publishing and building an author platform.

"We live and breathe words.... It was books that made me feel that perhaps I was not completely alone. They could be honest with me, and I with them. Reading your words, what you wrote, how you were lonely sometimes and afraid, but always brave; the way you saw the world, its colors and textures and sounds, I felt--I felt the way you thought, hoped, felt, dreamt. I felt I was dreaming and thinking and feeling with you. I dreamed what you dreamed, wanted what you wanted--and then I realized that truly I just wanted you."

— **Cassandra Clare,** *Clockwork Prince*

Conclusion: Writing Beyond Rejection

"I don't care if a reader hates one of my stories, just as long as he finishes the book."

—Roald Dahl

We have almost come to the end of *Rejection Free For Writers*. I certainly hope you enjoyed the book and gained the confidence to write and publish your own work.

You are destined to do great things with your life, and I believe in you and your dream to be a successful writer.

After reading this book, I hope you're feeling inspired to write full-time. Or maybe you just want to earn extra income to take your kids to Disneyland. Whatever your reasons, writing can provide you with a new way of life. It can take you deep into the mind of a character you create, or it can help you build an online business.

Whatever path you take, make sure it's in an area of your expertise that you can talk about. People will ask you questions later. You'll get fan mail. You might have interviews or be featured on CNN. The sky is the limit with the only limitations being the limits you set for yourself. This not only pertains to writing, but pretty much everything in life. You get what you put into it.

If you give your writing the attention it deserves and stick with a daily schedule, you can have the dream. Writing and publishing are exciting avenues to take. It's not for everyone, but rather, for a select few. We can make our dreams happen if we work toward that dream relentlessly.

There is a lot of potential in the power of resilience. It can change everything. Do what you love and do it better than anyone. Naysayers might ask questions like, "Have you sold any books yet?" or "Have you quit your job to write?"

Just remember you're writing your way to freedom. The way to that freedom is through the fears holding you down. I hope this book has given you the tools to face that fear and smile. You know you have what it takes. You made it this far. Now take it the rest of the way.

Rejection is part of the growth process. You need it to push into the areas you fear. That is where real growth takes place.

Self-doubt and uncertainty are natural feelings when trying something new. Let these emotions happen, but don't give them permission to control you.

Rejecting Rejection and Embracing the Writer Within

Throughout this book, we discussed authors who were rejected dozens of times by the publishers and editors who judged the work as not meeting industry standards or current trends. If these authors had listened to the critics and given up, chances are we would have missed out on a good deal of literary brilliance.

These authors had to struggle with a lot of self-rejection. Did they want to give up? Maybe. Did they carry a burden of self-doubt? Most likely. But the one thing they had in common was that they learned how to influence the power of rejecting rejection.

This is when we stand up to the critics, judges, and the voices inside our own mind. We push back and say, "No, I will not let you win today." We decide again and again that we are authors and that, no matter what, we can persevere. It doesn't matter if you plan to write just one book or a dozen. You have the choice to give in or push on.

Reject the doubters in your mind. Reject the rejection when it tells you to quit. Reject the critics who tell you that your writing is no good. Opinions always vary.

Write what you love and write from the heart. Don't simply write what others want to hear. You might work for years and get nothing. Then, one day, when the last mile is in sight and you think you can't push on anymore, that's when the journey starts to make sense.

Will you give up today or do you have a little more fight in you? When you realize the struggle was the best part, then we can appreciate what it takes to write a book. When your words are read by those who need a book like yours, then you can take a break—until the next book.

Writers are people who write.

So, what are you waiting for?

It's time to build your dream of being that writer.

Scott Allan

scottallan@scottallanpublishing.com

"Close the door. Write with no one looking over your shoulder. Don't try to figure out what other people want to hear from you; figure out what you have to say. It's the one and only thing you have to offer.

—Barbara Kingsolver

Download this _Free Training_ Guide—Built For
Stealth: Key Principles for Building a Great Life

_Available wherever **books**, **eBooks** and
audiobooks are sold._

Books Change Lives.
Let's Change Yours Today.

Check out the complete
Bulletproof Mindset Mastery series here by Scott Allan.

Visit author.to/ScottAllanBooks or scan the QR Code below to
follow Scott Allan and stay up to date on future book releases

The **Rejection Free for Life**
Series Books

Begin Your Rejection Free Journey Today!

RejectionFreeBooks.com

Pathways to Mastery Series

Master Your Life One Book at a Time

Available where eBooks, books and audiobooks are sold.

About Scott Allan

Scott Allan is an international bestselling author of 25+ books published in 7 languages in the area of personal growth and self-development. He is the author of **Fail Big**, **Undefeated**, and **Do the Hard Things First**.

As a former corporate business trainer in Japan, and **Transformational Mindset Strategist**, Scott has invested over 10,000 hours of research and instructional coaching into the areas of self-mastery and leadership training.

With an unrelenting passion for teaching, building critical life skills, and inspiring people around the world to take charge of their lives, Scott Allan is committed to a path of **constant and never-ending self-improvement**.

Many of the success strategies and self-empowerment material that is reinventing lives around the world evolves from Scott Allan's 20 years of practice and teaching critical skills to corporate executives, individuals, and business owners.

You can connect with Scott at:

scottallan@scottallanpublishing.com

Visit author.to/ScottAllanBooks to stay up to date on future book releases.

Scott Allan

Master Your Life One Book at a Time.